Operational Research
for Managers

Philip Allan textbooks in Business Studies

Consulting Editors:

BRYAN CARSBERG
Professor of Accounting, University of Manchester

W DUNCAN REEKIE
Lecturer in Business Policy, University of Edinburgh

RAYMOND THOMAS
Professor of Business Administration, University of Bath

Operational Research for Managers

EDITED BY:

S C Littlechild

Professor of Commerce, University of Birmingham

Philip Allan

First published 1977 by

PHILIP ALLAN PUBLISHERS LIMITED
MARKET PLACE
DEDDINGTON
OXFORD OX5 4SE

0 86003 504 2 (hardback)
0 86003 604 9 (paperback)

Reprinted 1978, 1980, 1984, 1988

Set by Preface Ltd, Salisbury
Printed in Great Britain by The Camelot Press Limited, Southampton

Contents

Preface

There are now many excellent books on operational research. However, these books fall almost entirely into one of two categories: the relatively brief, non-technical appreciation for the manager and intelligent layman (e.g. the books by Duckworth or Rivett and Ackoff) or the more voluminous mathematical treatments of techniques for the specialist (e.g. those by Wagner or Hillier and Lieberman).* There is hardly any choice of text at all for the numerous engineers, economists and accountants, whether undergraduate students or practising managers, who do not intend to become operational research practitioners, but who wish to gain a more thorough introduction to the techniques and practice of operational research than the appreciation books provide. *Operational Research for Managers* is intended to fill this gap.

The book originated in a 30-hour course of lectures given to young executives attending the six-month Diploma in Business Administration course at the University of Aston Management Centre. Lectures by members of the Centre staff were supplemented by seminars on actual applications led by visitors from industrial operational research groups. In this way, the practical advantages and disadvantages of each operational

*Duckworth W. E., *A Guide to Operational Research*, Methuen 1962. Hillier F. and Lieberman G. J., *Introduction to Operations Research*, Holden Day 1967. Rivett P. and Ackoff R. L., *A Managers Guide to Operational Research*, Wiley 1963. Wagner H. M., *Principles of Management Science* and *Principles of Operations Research*, Prentice Hall 1970.

research technique were communicated, along with a feeling for 'what it is all about'. Since weekly visits from practising operational research managers and consultants are not generally feasible for most lecture courses, it seemed worth trying to embody our experience in a text which could be used much more widely. The present volume is the result. It consists of chapters on theory alternating with case studies illustrating how the theory has been applied in industry.

The emphasis is therefore on techniques which have been repeatedly found to be useful in practice, rather than on techniques which are merely elegant or attractive in theory. This explains the omission of topics such as game theory. Other topics such as reliability, maintenance and dynamic programming have been omitted partly because of their relatively narrow special interest and partly because of the relatively advanced statistical techniques required.

Reflecting the above philosophy, a unique feature of the book is the emphasis on implementation. For too many students, operational research appears to be nothing more than a collection of theoretical techniques. Such students find great difficulty in usefully relating these techniques to the real-world problems which they subsequently encounter. Our book as a whole is an attempt to show how theoretical techniques are modified when put into practice. The last chapter, entitled 'Putting operational research to work', discusses how operational research groups go about the business of finding problems, what balance of skills is required and what organisational structures within the firm are most conducive to success.

Operational Research for Managers is designed for use both by experienced managers and by potential managers still studying for their qualifications (whether diplomas, first degrees or higher degrees). It is suitable for courses ranging from 10 to 50 hours in length. At the shorter end of the scale, a brief appreciation of OR can be based on the eight case studies and the introductory and concluding chapters, with the theory chapters available to any manager with an interest in a particular technique. At the longer end of the scale, the theory chapters provide a basic grounding in technique which has been designed in the light of curricula at universities and polytechnics, and the requirements of various professional bodies. For the latter purposes exercises

have been provided after each chapter. An Instructor's Manual
is also available. Following each chapter is a collection of
references and suggestions for further reading.

The book requires no mathematical knowledge beyond GCE
'O' level. Calculus is used only once, in the derivation of the
economic order quantity. However, some familiarity with
elementary statistics is assumed — specifically, with the
following concepts: subscript and summation notation; mean,
standard deviation, frequency distribution, histogram, random
variable, percentile; normal and Poisson distributions;
significance tests and hypothesis testing; simple and conditional
probabilities. It will surely be the case that a suitable
introduction to statistics will be given at the same time as, or
just before, a course in operational research. The concept of net
present value is also used on several occasions without further
explanation.

As editor, I have ruthlessly rewritten the contributions of the
various authors wherever it seemed necessary in order to achieve
a unified level and style. In this, I have been tremendously
helped by discussion with the contributing operational research
managers, by detailed written comments on the whole book from
C. R. Barrett and F. M. Wilkes, and by remarks on particular
chapters by P. G. Ascroft, S. I. Katz, H. Nicholls and J. R. Slater.

Any joint effort of this kind also depends upon secretarial
help from many people. I should particularly like to thank Kathy
Major, Helen Silk and Joy Tonkin for patiently retyping successive drafts of the whole book and fiercely chasing up laggardly
contributors.

S. C. Littlechild
Birmingham, September 1976

List of Contributors

D COMINS, OR Manager, Courtaulds Ltd.

S L COOK, Professor of OR, University of Aston Management Centre; formerly National Coal Board and OR Manager, Richard Thomas and Baldwins.

A M DUNSMUIR, Alfred Dunhill Ltd; formerly with Arthur Andersen & Co.

P G FITZGERALD, formerly OR Manager, GKN.

F GLOVER, Professor of Management Science, University of Colorado.

M J HARRISON, Consultant, Group Management Services, GKN.

D R KAYE, Partner, Arthur Andersen & Co.

J B KIDD, Lecturer in OR, University of Aston Management Centre; formerly with CEGB OR Group.

D D KLINGMAN, Professor of OR and Computer Sciences, University of Texas at Austin.

C D LEWIS, Professor of Operations Management, University of Aston Management Centre.

S C LITTLECHILD, Professor of Commerce, University of Birmingham; formerly Professor of Applied Economics, University of Aston Management Centre.

A W McCURDY, Leyland Cars.

M PIDD, Lecturer in OR, University of Aston Management Centre; formerly with Cadbury's OR Group.

R W PIPE, OR Manager, Cadbury Schweppes Ltd.

L B SPARROW, Corporate Planning Manager, West Midlands Gas.

N A SIMPSON, OR Department, CEGB Midlands Region

1

The History of Operational Research

S L COOK

1 Introduction

Operational research (OR) has been described as a method, an approach, a set of techniques, a team activity; a combination of many disciplines, an extension of particular disciplines (mathematics, engineering, economics), a new discipline; a vocation, even a religion. It is perhaps some of all these things. The best way to put the components in perspective, and perhaps the only definitive way of describing it, is to recount how it has evolved historically.

The idea of using 'scientific' approaches to resolve problems of design and decision has be ascribed to many thinkers in history, from Archimedes through Leonardo da Vinci to Charles Babbage in the last century. But for our purpose it is perhaps enough to go back to the 1930's. In that decade, a number of the eminent scientists in Britain, most of them Fellows of the Royal Society, came to believe that science had taken a wrong turning. Pure science, the search for knowledge for its own sake, was esteemed above applied science and engineering — the application of scientific knowledge and scientific method to the problems of man and society.

2   The Call to Arms

New ideas do not automatically lead to action; but in the mid-1930's there was developing a sense of national and international emergency over the threat from Nazi Germany. Already, Robert Watson-Watt was leading a group of scientists and technologists in the development of radar, in great secrecy, for the defence of Britain against air attack. The approaching second world war, and the war itself, provided the opportunity for the application of science on an unprecedented scale in the service of national objectives. In the course of this, OR under that name emerged as a specific scientific activity, first in Britain and then in the United States and Canada. We cannot go into the full story here, and a few key events must suffice.

Watson-Watt and his colleagues in 1937 were ready to demonstrate to the Armed Forces the application of their prototype radar equipment to the detection of approaching enemy aircraft and the deployment of anti-aircraft batteries and fighter planes to repel them. The first large scale trials, however, had disappointing results, and the defence chiefs asked Watson-Watt to make a special study of the results of the trials and of the problems of using the equipment in real-life conditions. He selected from his group a small team of half a dozen, with a range of disciplines including physics, electronics, mathematics, statistics and psychology. The team came up with analyses of two particular man-machine interfaces: that of the service operators of the radar equipment, indicating how they might be trained to use it more effectively, and that of the service officers interpreting the information obtained from the equipment for the development of anti-aircraft guns and fighters, showing how this information could be converted to effective defensive tactics for a particular offensive situation.

Subsequent trials after implementation of the recommendations were much more effective, and the defence chiefs asked for the team to be kept in being to monitor the continuing development of radar. The team was given an office in Operational Headquarters, where it remained until radar was proving its value in the Battle of Britain in 1940. To identify the room and the non-uniformed scientists using it, the phrase 'operational research' was coined for the six-man team, and the door labelled to that effect. It meant 'research into operations', or perhaps 'research within operational headquarters'. It carried no broader connotations.

In 1939 Professor Patrick Blackett, the physicist, who was already famous for his work in the field of relativity, and who had been a naval officer during the first world war, offered his services as a scientific advisor to the admiralty. He was involved in a number of crucial tactical and strategic issues to do with the Battle of the Atlantic, of which the best known are probably those concerned with the number of merchant ships and escort vessels in an Atlantic convoy, and the tactics of Coastal Command in seeking out and destroying U-boats around the coast. At the same time, Professor J. D. Bernal was advising the Home Office on the defence of the civil population against air raids, and other eminent scientists were becoming similarly involved.

Up to this point, the various initiatives were separate attempts to offer scientific support to the defence services, but in 1940 Blackett and the others realised that this work involved a new kind of activity with a common thread running through it. They sought a name for it, which could be used in discussions with government to encourage its increased development and use in the war effort. Watson-Watt suggested that the label 'operational research' which had remained serviceable for three years for his team, might be adopted to describe the general activity, and it was agreed.

The United States, already deeply committed to supporting Britain with food and supplies, was moving towards full involvement in the war. Blackett wrote to his friend and fellow professor of physics at the Massachusetts Institute of Technology in Boston, Philip Morse, to tell him of the way science was aiding the war effort in Britain and to suggest that something similar might be done in the USA. Morse was able to arrange for a special conference in the USA of defence chiefs and scientists to which Blackett and some of his colleagues were flown by special plane. The Americans adopted the idea and the name, changing it only to 'operations research' because of their different usage of adjectival nouns. They quickly set up groups of OR scientists for the various branches of the armed forces, and throughout most of the war there were OR groups serving with the land, sea and air forces of Britain, Canada and the USA.[9,12,14]

3   Swords to plough shares

By the end of the war there were about one thousand scientists serving in the United States forces and a little over 200 in Britain. They came from a wide range of disciplines but mainly the physical and the life sciences, with a very few psychologists. They had, of course, been entirely concerned with military problems, and it would have been understandable if the new activity had become recognised simply as a new branch of military science or logistics. However, some of the leading scientists concerned were convinced that OR could be at least as valuable in peace as it had been in war; the greatest impetus in this direction came, once again, in Britain, with the radical programme of reconstruction and reform following the war.

This created a sense of urgency for the peace-time application of science comparable to that felt 10 years earlier with the approach of war. Several factors contributed to a rapid building up of OR in British industry in the late 1940's. First, the nationalisation programme of the new Labour Government created large industrial corporations (coal, steel, gas, electricity, road, rail and air transport), some much larger than any previous industrial organisations and with unprecedented problems of reconstruction and development. Second, some of the leaders of these corporations came from government or defence positions where they had experienced OR help with strategy and tactics during the war. Third, some of the leading defence OR scientists chose to move to industry after the war rather than return to their original disciplines and careers.

The quick and effective establishment of OR groups in these and other industries was helped by two other factors. First, tens of thousands of scientists and technologists were being demobilised from the defence research establishments and looking for jobs where they could find the same kind of challenge that they had found in war time. Most of them had not known of OR during the war, since the secret was well kept, but now they began to hear of it and many were attracted to it. There was also a major campaign by leading scientists in the two or three years following the war — 'Science and Reconstruction' — to persuade scientists and politicians that science should never again become a purely backroom operation, but that it should be fully harnessed to the needs of the country and the development of a better society. This missionary zeal was particularly evident in the early groups in the nationalised industries, and remains an important factor: enthusiasm is an essential element of successful OR work.

In the years 1947 to 1955, OR groups grew to play a major part in the development of most of the basic industries in Britain which had been nationalised. OR also began to spread in a smaller way to private industry, but the two largest groupings were in the coal[13] and steel[7] industries which had a major influence on the development of OR in Britain well into the 1960's.

4   OR in the USA

The initial post-war development of OR in the USA took place mainly in universities, in several important cases partially financed by the armed services, notably at Massachusetts Institute of Technology (US Navy), Johns Hopkins University (US Army) and University of California and RAND Corporation (US Airforce). From these three activities developed the impressive lead of the United States in the advanced mathematical techniques of operational research, particularly those based on mathematical probability and mathematical programming.

But it was a development from an altogether different direction which established the main basis for teaching the method of operational research and for developing the philosophy of the subject. In the late 1940's two young men who had obtained their doctorates in the philosophy of science in the University of Pennsylvania began to read of wartime OR and recognised it as, in principle, the combination of theory and action they had been seeking — the 'applied philosophy of science'. They visited a number of larger universities in the search for one which would sponsor an OR activity on these lines and eventually found it in the Case Institute of Technology in Cleveland, Ohio. The two men were C. West Churchman and Russell Ackoff. They joined the university, and recruited a number of interdisciplinary like-minded people forming a faculty OR group which quickly grew to a dozen members. At the same time, they obtained wide-spread support from industrial organisations to carry out OR studies on a consultancy basis. They launched a master's course in OR and offered part-time research assistant posts to students, who assisted with the consultancy assignments and were allowed to use the material from the assignments in their dissertations. In this way the teaching was geared very firmly to 'real-world' problem solving.

At the same time they had to set up course work programmes for the students in methods and relevant techniques. They based the teaching of method on their earlier work in the philosophy of science which they related closely to the practical stages of problem solving as they emerged from the work undertaken. For techniques, they took a range of those which had been used in one way or another in defence OR, and other techniques such as linear programming which had developed in business schools or in industrial engineering. With their wide range of consultancy opportunities they were able to select projects which would provide vehicles for the systematic development and application of particular techniques, and in this way, to develop material for teaching techniques and their areas of application at an increasingly advanced level. By 1956 they were able to publish the first textbook of OR, *Introduction to Operations Research*.[6]

Of all those early teachers of OR at the universities, Churchman and Ackoff were probably the most insistent that OR is a basic method and approach rather than a set of techniques. Nevertheless, the appearance of their book, a large part of which was inevitably concerned with specific techniques and their applications, probably helped to develop the idea in the world at large that OR was mainly a set of techniques. The method and approach were not so easy to describe in a distinctive way; the techniques by contrast were completely tangible. Many who had up to then found it difficult to appreciate the nature of OR were happy to seize on the techniques as if they defined the subject, and this difficulty has remained until the present day.

The early divergence of emphasis in the development of OR between the problem-oriented industry-based groups of the UK and the more technique-oriented university-based groups of the USA was moderated considerably in the 1960's. Several leading UK universities set up OR departments and practising OR groups spread rapidly in US industry. These developments were helped by exchanges of people and ideas which began in 1954. Nevertheless, it remains true that British 'operational research' is more practical and problem-based, while American 'operations research' tends to be seen by many as a form of applied mathematics.

5   The interdisciplinary group

Very soon in the development of OR, the practice emerged of analysis by teams, rather than by individuals, however, brilliant. At first, except for the Watson-Watt story, scientists were brought together regardless of their particular disciplines, but it was soon realised that a team containing a range of disciplines was more creative and more effective, with a wider range of potential approaches to a given problem, than one with its strength mainly in, say, physics or mathematics or biology. As the OR groups grew in size, the interactions between project teams as well as within teams was found to help creativity. The post-war industrial groups maintained this interdisciplinary approach. There were perhaps rather less biologists and psychologists (a loss, as we now well realise) but rather more engineers (research minded electricals, mechanicals and civils), metallurgists and mining engineers, and (for the first time) a very few economists.

A particularly useful interaction between engineers and statisticians marked the early post-war years. Project teams were seldom more than three or four strong, but never less than two (almost always of different disciplines). Occasionally an individual would have special responsibility for a part of the project, geared to his own discipline, but generally 'interdisciplinarity' was taken to mean that all team members should be concerned with all major aspects of the problem.

In the mid-1950's it came to be realised that an OR group of this kind was more than just a problem-solving resource; it was also a 'learning system', a vehicle for developing very rapidly the problem-solving competence of its members, in fact 'a miniature university' within its host organisation. Not surprisingly, perhaps, these groups did not always sit naturally in the organisation structure, being usually more radical, more innovative, less observant of the rule book and, at least apparently, less disciplined than other parts of the organisation. Thus the major groups during this period provided both the development laboratory for OR itself and the training ground for its practitioners.

6   Limitations of operational research

There is not space to describe here how operational research relates to various other disciplines such as systems science, cybernetics or management science, with all of which it has considerable overlap;[1-5, 8, 10, 11, 15] nor how it relates to the various other professional activities assisting the management process, such as work study, organisation and methods and systems analysis. There is not time to trace the growth of applications in government, notably in the health services, transport planning, local government, law enforcement, environmental management; nor the growth in aspirations of operational researchers to move towards tackling some of the most taxing problems of present day society, such as industrial or international conflict, aid to the third world or the relation between economic growth and the quality of life.

However, this growth in aspirations of the OR community can perhaps be mistaken for a lack of modesty about the present competence of OR to deal with such difficult questions. Some readers may feel that OR seems to be an insufferably arrogant profession, the only body able and willing (when it gets around to it) to solve humanity's great problems. Other readers, taking a kinder view, may see it as possibly competent, but by now rather removed in its concerns from the difficult but more mundane immediate problems of business and industry, and therefore unable to be of much help to today's managers. We should take a page or two to consider these criticisms.

It must be admitted that OR and the OR profession have limitations. OR is basically a research approach, which relies on individual flair, and competence varies widely between practitioners. It has no clear approach as yet to problems of multiple objectives, or where many independent decision makers are involved.

Again, time or cost place severe limits on the extent to which explicit and thorough analysis can be applied to every decision. This means that most smaller decisions will continue to be made intuitively by the manager, with insufficient information and little or no analysis; and this means that analysis for the larger decisions must take account of this fact. OR is not yet very skilled at making this allowance. Most of all, OR still lacks sufficient understanding of the behavioural sciences. (Even more perhaps, the behavioural sciences lack sufficient understanding of behaviour; but that is no excuse for ignoring the understanding they do already have.)

OR, like applied sciences in general and also like management, has to get on with the job and do the best it can. Decisions cannot wait until appropriate knowledge comes into existence. Thus the OR scientist must go about his job with humility not only concerning his own skills but concerning the subject he practices.

One might fear that, with its ever developing broad social interests, OR might no longer be interested in and therefore competent to tackle business and industrial problems. It is true that there has been some falling off of interest in industrial OR in the past decade, but this should be a temporary situation for three reasons:

1   In many of the developed countries (especially in the UK) the improvement of productivity in business and industry came for a time to be seen as of less importance than many other issues such as the environment, conservation of resources and development of social services. This is no longer true; productivity is seen to be vital to these other concerns.

2   Business and industry came to be buffeted by short-term influences of an apparently unpredictable kind, from finance,

from the market and from the trade unions. In this situation, reflective medium- and long-range planning of the kind to which OR could best contribute appeared to become irrelevant. Short-term 'seat of the pants' decision-making became the main mode of management, giving little encouragement to OR; furthermore, short-term economies could be made by reducing expenditure on OR. This was especially true where OR geared to cost reduction and efficient operation had been put aside in favour of OR for expansion. Sooner, rather than later, management must surely return to a modicum of reflective, longer range decision-making where OR can again be of particular benefit.

3 Some of the reasons for the 'buffeting' environment, and some serious blocks against solving the efficiency problems, are seen to be due to the lack of rational analysis and coherent social policy in the environment in which industry has to operate. (We include here, for example, the atmosphere affecting industrial relations.) Increased application of OR and other rational and reflective approaches to these broader problems should increase the confidence with which the problems within industry can themselves be tackled, and this can lead to greater interest in management for OR, and in OR people for work in industry.

For these reasons, any management showing enthusiasm for the development of creative and effective OR in its organisation should have no difficulty in attracting competent and well motivated OR scientists.

7 'Operational research for managers?'

So we come round to the theme of this book — OR for managers. What do we mean exactly?

We hope we have already established that OR is sufficiently interesting and perhaps sufficiently important for managers to want to know something about it as general background — especially if they may find themselves working with OR scientists. As we try to show in Chapter 19, for OR scientists and managers to work effectively in partnership each needs to have a good understanding of the others' methods, beliefs and tasks.

But is there another possibility? The manager can become, if he wishes, something of an operational researcher himself. All that is needed is the inclination, the time to pull out of day-to-day preoccupations (not perhaps so easy) and some minimum background in quantitative methods and scientific thinking. In Chapter 19 we discuss various ways in which this can be done without the full support of an OR group. There is in any case a wide range of OR applications. Some kinds are no longer 'research', and this includes many semi-routine applications of some of the techniques in this book. With a little expert guidance, some of these can provide a straightforward task for the manager, who may even be able to do a better job than the professional because of his local knowledge and availability for follow-up.

References and further reading

1   Ashby W. R., *Design for a Brain*, Chapman and Hall 1952 and 1960.

2   Beer S., 'What has cybernetics to do with operational research?' *OR Quarterly*, vol. 10, no. 1, March 1959.

3   Beer S., *Decision and Control*, Wiley 1966.

4   Beer S., *Platform for Change*, Wiley 1975.

5   Beishon J. and Peters G., *Systems Behaviour*, Open University 1972.

6   Churchman C. W., Ackoff R. and Arnoff L. E., *Introduction to Operations Research*, Wiley 1957.

7   Cook S. L., 'OR in steel', in D. B. Hertz and R. T. Eddison (eds), *Progress in OR*, vol. 2, Wiley 1964.

8   Forrester J., *Industrial Dynamics*, MIT Wiley 1961.

9   Gray G. W., *Science at War*, Books for Libraries 1943.

10   Heald G., *Approaches to the Study of Organisational Behaviour – OR in the Behavioural Sciences*, Tavistock 1970.

11   Lawrence J. D., *Operational Research and the Social Sciences*, Tavistock 1966.

12   Rivett B. H. P., *Concepts of Operational Research*, English Universities Press 1968.

13   Rivett B. H. P. and Cook S. L., Two chapters on 'OR in coal-mining', in J. F. McCloskey and J. M. Coppinger (eds), *Operations Research for Management*, vol. 2, Johns Hopkins Press 1955.

14   Waddington C. H., *OR in World War II — Operational Research Against the U-Boat*, Paul Elek 1973.

15   Wiener N., *Cybernetics*, MIT Press 1961.

2
The Operational Research Method

M PIDD

1 Introduction

Most of the chapters in this book are concerned with the theory or practice of particular OR techniques. From the point of view of the student this is sensible because it allows him (or her) to concentrate on one relatively self-contained topic at a time. In practice, however, a technique-dominated approach has disadvantages. It is extremely rare for any problem to come prepacked and labelled with 'linear programming' or 'network analysis'. Indeed, when work begins, it may not be very clear what the problem is, let alone how it should be solved.

Operational researchers have always been conscious that the problem should come first, not the technique. In the early days this was necessarily so because the techniques were rudimentary at best. But even now, when the analyst has a whole arsenal of mathematical methods and computer programmes at his disposal, he needs to be aware that the recognition of what the problem really is, and the practical implementation of a suitable solution, are at least as important as the technique used to obtain the solution.

There has been considerable interest, therefore, in developing a methodology of operational research — that is, a systematic procedure to be used in tackling OR problems. Notable contributions to such a methodology are to be found in the first major 'textbook' by Churchman, Ackoff and Arnoff,[4] and in the later work by Ackoff and Sasieni.[2] The 'hypothetico-deductive method' of Karl Popper[5] has also been influential. This combination is embodied in the-step-by step procedure described in this chapter. The description is inevitably over-simplified, but it does reflect the need to take a broad look at the problem and to structure the model before collecting data. The data are used to test and refine the model before developing strategies to deal with the problem.

2   The place of a methodology

As soon as one begins to formalise a methodology, it immediately becomes apparent that no two people tend to go about the same problem in exactly the same way. Hence, any set of prescriptions for problem-solving cannot be meant for robot-like application. They will need modification according to several distinct factors:

(a)   the personality of the researcher — for example, some people seem to be able to carry out several activities at the same time, whereas others prefer to operate strictly sequentially;

(b)   the type of problem under scrutiny — if it is known fairly well what the problem is before OR work begins, or if there have been similar applications, then short cuts may be possible;

(c)   the resources available — it is generally possible to produce a better solution given more time, more cash, more people or a bigger computer. The availability of such resources will determine how long the OR team is able (and willing) to spend on the different phases of their study.

Despite these modifications it is still worth considering how an OR worker usually tackles a project, narrows it to some-thing manageable and produces useful findings which are implemented. Of course, in this respect there may be nothing unique about the OR worker as distinct from, say, a systems engineer or a normal scientific research worker. However, the range of problems with which the OR analyst is confronted, and his responsibility for producing and implementing a solution, mean that the techniques themselves play a relatively smaller part in this work and the more general methodological aspects attain a correspondingly greater importance.

It may be asked whether a formal methodology is useful. Perhaps some people are just good at OR and others not. No doubt there is some truth in this, but there are two main reasons why following a methodology is useful:

1   It helps in training — in many medical schools, when the students first begin to examine patients, they are given a long check list of questions to ask and of areas to prod and tap. Initially, they need to follow such a list explicitly, but as their experience and confidence develop, they are able to modify it to suit their own personalities. They may even be able to take short cuts, but this can be dangerous. Similarly, students of OR may find it helpful to use a methodology as a sort of check-list which they go through whilst learning to deal with the sorts of problems which typify OR. Later on, they will develop their own personal approach which is more satisfactory.

2   It aids communication — large-scale projects are often tackled by teams which may consist of up to eight members. Obviously, they will function better if they have agreed goals as a group and have also agreed how they will go about reaching them. This implies that there is a need for the group to follow a methodology so that they can communicate effectively with one another about the current status of their work.

This second point also suggests why it is useful for the general manager to have an understanding of the OR methodology.

3   Summary of the methodology

An OR study usually involves the following ten stages:

1   describe problem in its context
2   collect preliminary information
3   define problem explicitly

4   set study objectives
5   formulate the OR problems
6   construct model
7   collect detailed data
8   test model
9   select solution from alternatives
10   implement and monitor solution.

As mentioned in the previous section, different analysts might add or subtract certain stages, but the above stages would usually be followed in the order given. It should be emphasised, however, that it is not necessary to complete each stage before moving on to the next — in practice, several stages will overlap. Several stages are likely to be approached in the light of what will happen at future stages (e.g. data availability or solution requirements). There will generally be a degree of 'back-tracking' as information gained in the course of the study throws new light on a previous stage. Thus, it may well be found that the real nature of a problem is rather different from what it initially seemed to be, hence different kinds of data need to be collected. These points will become evident as the chapter progresses.

The methodology attempts to consider the problem in its context before narrowing down to what can be actively tackled in the project. It does this because of a fundamental idea about the nature of problems — they have no explicit existence in their own right! What actually exists is some dissatisfaction with the current state of affairs (where this can include designs for the future), and what the OR worker must do is examine the situation to see how the relevant factors interact. From this he may then be in a position to state tentative ideas about the nature of the problem which underlies the dissatisfaction. How the problem is defined may well depend on the interests and viewpoint of the researcher. His prior experience may cause the intuitive rejection of certain ideas about the nature of the problem, though different workers might well accept these ideas as reasonable.

It is worth mentioning that the manager responsible for a particular problem area may not recognise that he has a problem, or may not be willing to acknowledge its existence. In practice, only a part of any OR group's work comes from spontaneous requests by management. A sizeable part of the work comes from projects proposed by the OR group itself and 'sold' to managers. Thus the implementation of OR, in the broad sense, includes the identification of OR problems. This issue is discussed at some length in the final chapter.

Once a problem has been identified, it is examined in more detail and an abstract model, meant to represent its important features, is developed. The model is then used to test out various strategies (of which there may be almost an infinite number) to find the one which is in some sense the best. If this solution is acceptable, it is implemented and the situation monitored carefully to ensure that the expected improvement in performance actually accrues. It is often not as simple as this account suggests, because the initial dissatisfaction may have been caused by a set of interlinked 'problems' which all need to be solved. In such situations, the OR worker needs to be much more creative and the work involved is much more difficult.

The next ten sections of this chapter explore in greater detail the stages listed at the beginning of the present section. It is only fair to warn the reader that until he has attempted to formulate and solve OR problems himself, he may not appreciate the full significance of this methodology. Rather than carefully study the chapter now, the reader would be better advised to read the chapter once, to get the flavour of the approach, and to return to it towards the end of his course, or when he is faced with a difficult problem.

4   Stage 1: contextual investigation

As mentioned earlier, the trouble with problems is that, like beauty, they exist in the eye of the beholder. The aim of the first few phases is to root out a manageable OR problem from the initial unsatisfactory state of affairs. In this phase it can be helpful to draw what are often called **system maps** which usually take the form of **influence diagrams** (though by no means all practitioners do this). As is suggested by their name, influence diagrams attempt to show all the influences at work in a particular situation. Initially there is no attempt to show the way these influences operate, but the diagram may well reveal any hierarchies which exist. It is, of course, possible to write down verbally the content of an influence diagram — however, if the relationships are at all complex, the diagrammatic representation will generally be much easier to follow. An added advantage is that it is also quicker to construct and easier to modify.

Suppose a manager in a biscuit factory calls in an OR team because he is unhappy about the way his investment in material stocks always seems to be high and yet the factory floor seems to be without stock materials on occasions. The OR team talks with the factory manager, one or two of his staff, the purchasing manager and also the marketing manager. These discussions lead them to construct the sequence of influence diagrams shown in figure 1.

The first influence diagram, figure 1(a), is extremely simple and shows only the obvious. It shows three systems; the central one is the factory system which is shown as having three components relevant to the unsatisfactory situation. (Note that the size of this set is an arbitrary decision by the researchers.) Outside the factory system, but influencing its behaviour, are the supplies policy and the marketing policy of the organisation.

Further thought and discussion allows the researchers to lump together the production and finished goods components, figure 1(b), but to split the raw stock component into the material itself, a system for controlling these and the space needed. Similarly, the purchasing policy can be explicitly divided to show the availability of supplies and the cost of capital tied up in stocks.

Now it should be obvious that a long sequence of such diagrams of ever-increasing complexity could be drawn to show the influence at work in a situation. For the purposes of this account it is sufficient to stop at this point, but the reader should notice one potential advantage of this type of approach. It allows the researchers to talk easily with the managers, because the diagram is not mathematical and is easily understood by most people. Hence, right at the start of the project the process of understanding that is essential to successful implementation can begin.

(a) Outline diagram

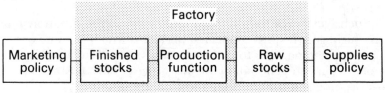

(b) Second diagram

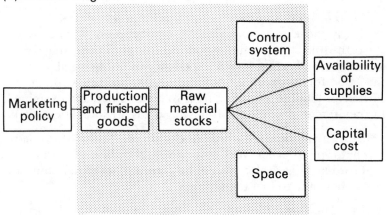

Figure 1. Influence diagrams

5   Stage 2: preliminary information collection

Sooner or later, the process of drawing the influence diagram
leads to a need for more information. This does not imply that
a detailed data collection exercise is necessary at this phase, but,
for example, it would be sensible for the research team in our
hypothetical exercise to do the following. First they should
briefly examine the range of the raw stock carried in the
factory — is it homogeneous or can it be divided up in an A-B-C
type classification? (See Chapters 10 and 11 on forecasting and
stock control.) Second, they should investigate a few of the

recent crises that precipitated the call of the factory manager for help.

Such *brief* investigations shed more light on the situation and also highlight the interconnected problems which lie at its core. They make it possible to complete the system map in rather more detail and hence allow the next phase. This illustrates the overlapping and backtracking mentioned earlier.

6   Stage 3: explicit problem definition

The researcher should now be in a position to define explicitly those areas on which some rather more detailed work is worthwhile. The point about doing things in this sequence is to avoid the all-too-common experience of not being able to see the wood for the trees. We have now described the wood in sufficient detail to allow the trees to be specified and examined. In the present example the following areas might be identified:

(a)   The method by which stocks are physically controlled: what type of paper work system would be best and what record-keeping system would be accurate, up-to-date but not cumbersome to maintain?

(b)   The flow of information from the marketing department to the factory: is there any way of formalising and controlling this so that the production and stock controllers are given sufficient notice of the running of promotions and special offers and the introduction of new packs?

(c)   The demand forecasts (on which the material requirements are calculated): are they accurate enough for effective planning? It may be worth installing a new mathematical forecasting method.

(d)   The ideal stock levels set by the stock policy may need to be revised and stock control theory may be useful here.

7   Stage 4: study objectives

An important stage in any research study, including OR, is the formulation of objectives for the project. Without these, terms of reference cannot be drawn up and it is impossible to judge whether the study is complete or successful. Having explicitly defined the problems to be considered, it is possible to set reasonable objectives which take account of the resources available to the team. As mentioned earlier, these include time, manpower, cash, computing facilities, etc., and the extent of these will affect the result which may reasonably be expected from the study.

For our example, a small team of three, which included an organisation and methods expert, might decide that all four areas mentioned in step 3 should be tackled. They might also go on to define how the factory manager can measure whether his production system functions better following their recommendations. Some research workers do not enjoy this phase of a project, arguing that if something really is research, then it must be a step into the unknown. This is true, but some standard procedures are necessary, just as an airline pilot might be delayed en route by winds, storms or congestion, but he still logs a flight plan before taking off.

8   Stage 5: problem formulation

Having defined the problems which need to be tackled and also having set reasonable objectives for the study, the OR team is now in a position to formulate the problems in terms which are amenable to the analysis which typifies OR. One of the characteristic ways in which OR is conducted is by the use of decision models; these will be discussed in the next phase of the methodology. If such models are to be used, then the problem needs to be set in a format which allows their development. Doing this is what is meant by problem formulation.

To formulate a problem for which a decision model is to be used, Ackoff and Sasieni[2] argue that we must answer five questions:

1   Who will make the decision? In the simplest cases this is obvious and may be the individual who called in the OR team in the first place, but on some occasions there can be multiple

decision makers (e.g. a committee) or there may be several 'stake-holders' who have conflicting objectives.

2   What are the objectives of the decision maker(s)? This question clearly cannot be answered without reference to question 1. The simplest formulations, such as those underlying the techniques described in the later chapters of this book, assume that there is a single decision maker with a straightforward single objective, such as maximising profit. Any attempt to allow for multiple conflicting objectives is usually tackled (in the use of these techniques) by treating one as a major objective and others as constraints on it. For our example, it is likely that the decision maker is the factory manager and that his objective is the achievement of desired levels of specified production at lowest possible total cost. Note that it is up to the OR worker to tease the objectives from the decision maker and not just to assume them in academic isolation.

3   Which relevant factors of the situation are subject to the control of the decision maker(s) (the controllable variables) and over what range may they be controlled? If the influence diagram has been drawn in sufficient detail, it may be possible to develop these from the influences shown on it. At this stage, there is no need to specify how these factors operate, but if this is known, then the information should be noted.

At this point, it becomes necessary in our example to think of at least two separate but linked problems, namely the problems of setting stock policies (levels and re-order intervals, etc.) and of forecasting the demand. For each the controllable factors should be listed.

4   What other aspects of the environment can affect the outcome of the available choices (the uncontrollable variables)? Again, the influence diagram will be a usual starting point in making such a list and in considering how these factors operate. Once again, in our example this would be done separately for the two related problems.

5   What decision criterion is appropriate? Ideally, the OR model should include an objective function which measures

the value of each alternative in terms of the objective(s) previously agreed. Without such a function, a linear programming model cannot proceed and it is also at the heart of the stock control theory discussed in Chapter 11.

It may become obvious at this stage that the preceding four stages have not been carried out in sufficient depth, in which case it may be necessary to backtrack and repeat them before the problem formulation is complete.

9   Stage 6: model construction

Most OR studies use a model of some sort during their efforts. In general terms, a model is simply a representation of reality which is used either to discover how to improve the real system or to discover what effect different policies will have on the real world. In constructing a model, the OR worker attempts to embody in some accurate representation what seem to be the important elements of the real-world situation (hence the significance of the problem formulation phase). In the simplest case, this representation might be a scale model, say of a factory layout, and at the other extreme could be a complex set of mathematical equations whose variables represent the controllable and uncontrollable factors acting in the situation.

In current operational research two types of model predominate. The first type uses mathematics to represent the relationships between the variables acting in a situation. Such models can sometimes be very simple and easy to understand (e.g. in the case of the basic stock control theory) and their elegance and clarity allows them to represent very complicated behaviour. The situations they represent are, of course, idealised. Most of the OR techniques described in this book are of this type. Obviously, it makes work easier if one of these techniques is applicable.

The second common type of model is usually called a **logical** model. These are most commonly used in simulation studies (see Chapters 15 and 16), and are reflected in the flow charts used to design a simulation model. There is less emphasis on mathematical equations than on representing the structure of a situation in such a way that the model may be manipulated.

It is possible to categorise models as optimising or merely descriptive: both types are widely used in OR. Mathematical models generally optimise, while logical methods describe. The aim of most OR studies is to aid the decision maker, and to do this the model may be used in two ways:

(a)   as a method of taking account of the preferences of the decision maker and all the factors at work so as to produce a single best solution. This optimum may then be tested to see how sensitive it is to changes in the values of the variables.

(b)   simply as a way of exploring what the likely effect will be of adopting a particular policy. This is, in effect, a simulation approach, though it need not necessarily follow the Monte Carlo pattern described in Chapter 15.

Whether the model is ultimately used to optimise or to explore is dependent on the nature of the study and not on the type of model.

10   Stage 7: detailed data collection

It is sometimes argued that scientists (whether in pure research or operational research) should first collect large amounts of data then analyse these to derive theories or models. Although this seems reasonable at first, it is currently believed that this approach puts the cart before the horse, and that it is the requirements of the theory or model which indicate what data should be collected (and, indeed, how accurate these data need be). Of course, one needs to have some familiarity with the situation in order to construct a relevant model (hence the preliminary information gathering at stage 2). In constructing the model, the good OR worker will do so with an eye to the data likely to be available or the experimentation which may be possible. Hence it may not be easy in practice to separate steps 6 and 7 as the limitations of data and the development of the model influence one another. Even if a model is constructed independently of the data, it will need to be modified if the data are unavailable. This emphasises the point, already made several times, that the step-by-step representation of a methodology is very limited, and backtracking is not only inevitable but desirable.

Intelligent data collection and collation require the OR worker to be familiar with statistical theory, but this is beyond the scope of this text.

11   Stage 8: model validation

Though this is shown as a distinct phase in the OR study, in reality the OR worker continually attempts to validate his work. At all stages, he has to compare his problem formulations and models with reality and discuss them with the project sponsors.

However, this is probably the most vexing part of any OR study and often the phase which gets the least attention. The aim is to develop and use a model which is a good representation of reality. The reason why it is so difficult hinges on those two words 'good' and 'reality': how good is 'good' and what do we mean by 'reality'?

There are several possibilities depending on the type of model under scrutiny. For a non-optimising, descriptive model its behaviour may be compared with that of the real system under similar conditions. If the behaviour is totally unlike it, then something is wrong — the data, the model, or both. For an optimising model the validation dilemma is rather different and will probably depend on the agreement of all the concerned parties that the model is reasonable. This may not sound very scientific, but it is better than just leaving it to the opinion of the researcher.

Notice that the idea of validation implies a purpose, and a model which is useful for one objective may be totally useless for another. One aspect of this is the level of detail of the model — one which is ideal in the total resources allocation of a business may be valueless in allocating those same resources within a factory.

12   Stage 9: solution choice

Given that the model has been agreed as valid, the next obvious step is to use the data available in the model to see what action should be taken. In the simple biscuit example, a fairly straightforward optimising model would probably have been used, in which case the data could be used to calculate the optimum solution. The data would also give an indication of how variable the factors were in reality and hence could also be used to see how sensitive this optimum turns out to be.

If the model is descriptive, then the data will be used as a mimic of the real situation. In this artificial environment, the model may be used to test the different options open to the decision maker. Indeed, the model may even be programmed on a computer and manipulated by the decision maker(s) using a terminal attached to the computer. In this type of situation, the decision maker selects the solution (i.e. policy) which best meets his objectives.

13   Stage 10: implementation

It is impossible in this type of phased description to find a reasonable place for the implementation of the operational research. Yet, any OR study is not judged ultimately on its technical or methodological sophistication but by its effect within the organisation. To improve the system under scrutiny, the solutions developed by the OR team must be implemented. However, this is rarely a one-shot exercise, nor does it happen solely at the end of the project. Parts of the solution may be developed and implemented in instalments, and in any case the development of the understanding needed for successful implementation begins as the OR team starts to work.

Chapter 19 discusses the ways in which operational research might be carried out. From these it is clear that implementation, and the control of the changes recommended, depends on close cooperation between the OR team and the functional management. Implementation begins in a sense only with cooperation when the OR team and the managers strive together to solve the problem. It does not begin (at all!) if the OR workers disappear for several months or years and reappear to confront management with 'the solution'.

Successful operational research always involves a process of learning, both on the part of the OR team and of the client.

This cannot happen if the two parties meet only at the start and finish of the project. Continual contact and review enables understanding and trust to be developed, so that the manager need not fear recommendations based on scientific 'mumbo-jumbo' which he does not understand. If, at the end of an operational research project, recommendations need to be 'sold' to a reluctant management, then there have been deficiencies in the conduct of the study.

Two other aspects of implementation that deserve mention concern the translation of theoretical results into actual practice within the organisation. First, it is often not possible directly to implement the recommendations. For example, a firm may carry out a large study to determine the most favourable geographical positions for its depots. However, it will clearly not be feasible to replace overnight the existing depots by new ones. Instead, a strategy of replacement needs to be develped which will avoid disruption of the firm's service to its customers and allow for any necessary staff training. The cost of this strategy needs to be carefully calculated to ensure that it does not exceed the benefits stemming from the change.

Second, conditions in an organisation do not stay the same; they vary through time and will certainly be different at the start and finish of the project. It is therefore important to develop a control system which ensures that the solution is adapted to meet changing circumstances. For example, Chapters 10 and 11 describe schemes for monitoring changes in demand and modifying inventory policy accordingly.

14   Concluding discussion

It is impossible in a chapter of this type to adequately convey the way an OR study is carried out. Rivett[6] asks 'What goes on in the mind of the OR scientist entering the soap factory for the first time?', and we may add 'and how are these thoughts developed into the final implemented solution?' Here we have only been able to show how one possible approach might work. Most of the features of this methodology are common to any logical sequence aimed at problem solving, and it would be surprising if this were not the case.

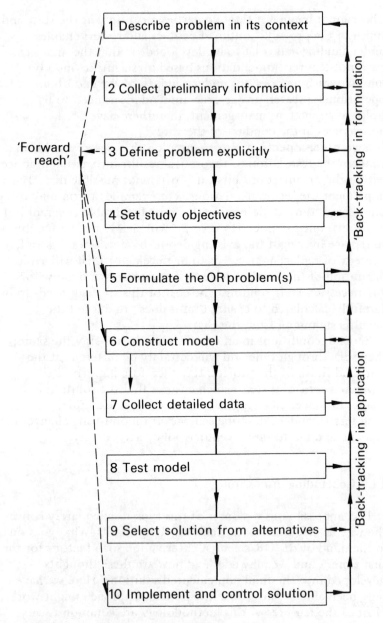

Figure 2. A more realistic OR methodology

It should by now be apparent why we have emphasised that the bare list of stages given in section 2 is inadequate and possibly misleading. The different stages are by no means clear cut and many of them overlap. Indeed, 'each phase usually continues until the project is completed and continuallly interacts with the others'.[2] Without being cynical, one might say that only when the project is finished does everyone know what the problem was (and possibly not even then). Second, there has to be some 'forward-reaching' because no early stage is carried out in complete ignorance of what the other stages may produce. In constructing the model the analyst will be aware of some of the data limitations even before the data collection phase has started. Finally, the approach is iterative or cyclic, with 'back-tracking' to carry out early stages several times because of what is discovered later on. Figure 2 is an attempt to show some of the rich interactions which exist in practice. All of the case study chapters, but particularly the next one, illustrate various aspects of this type of methodology in action.

References and further reading

1   Ackoff R. L., *Scientific Method: Optimising Applied Research Decisions*, Wiley 1962.

2   Ackoff R. L. and Sasieni, M., *Fundamentals of Operations Research*, Wiley 1968.

3   Churchman C. W., *The Systems Approach*, Dell 1968.

4   Churchman C. W., Ackoff R. L. and Arnoff L. E., *Introduction to Operations Research*, Wiley 1957.

5   Magee B., *Popper*, Fontana 1973.

6   Rivett B. H. P., *Concepts of Operational Research*, New Thinkers Library 1968.

3

A Transport and Distribution Study at Courtaulds

D COMINS

1 Introduction

In April 1973, the Operations Executive of Courtalds Limited decided to organise more efficient distribution of the Group's products and, as a first step, commissioned a study of its UK transport arrangements. A team was set up, drawing upon the resources of the OR department, with the addition of a full-time transport specialist, and reporting frequently to two senior executives of the Group, both of whom had a responsibility for an aspect of transport among their normal duties.

The instructions to the team were clear and straightforward – a detailed study was to be made of UK transport arrangements, including the utilisation of existing vehicles, arrangements with outside hauliers and the rates paid to them, and the way in which Group resources should be deployed to obtain maximum efficiency. Recommendations were expected within six months.

2 Review of methodology

Although OR projects vary in size from a few days' work for one person to those which occupy several people full-time for many months, they all need a disciplined approach to solving problems. Recall that the sequence of tasks on which the OR worker would expect to be engaged is, briefly:

(a)   to familiarise himself (or herself) with the system being studied; to identify the relevant factors affecting operations; and to define the problem in useful terms for analysis;
(b)   to collect and analyse relevant data using appropriate statistical and other quantitative techniques, and to formulate and test a practical solution;
(c)   to present convincing recommendations for action to the managers concerned, and to assist in implementing their decisions.

3   Background

The context of our work was that of a major British manufactoring company. Courtalds are pre-eminently a fibre and textile organisation, starting in the silk textile business early in the 19th century and pioneering the development of the man-made fibres industry from 1904 so that textile activities came to take second place. From the early 1960's, the balance again moved towards textiles, as the company's own textile capacity was expanded and garment and other manufactures incorporated into a unique, vertically integrated manufacturing and marketing organisation. In addition, Courtalds' interests cover six major related industries — chemicals, woodpulp, packaging materials, plastics, paint and engineering, and other activities such as farming. The Group has some 400 manufacturing units in the UK in 230 different locations.

4   Setting study objectives

The diversity of Courtalds' operations, the wide geographical scatter of factories and other despatch points, the complex flow of materials between localised, specialist producers (characteristic of the long chain of textile production processes), all combined to make a study of the whole system the only viable base for effective action.

The first and major problem was to devise a manageable programme of work which would enable sensible, practical recommendations to be submitted within the time limit. An elementary step was to consider the possible recommendations. It was apparent that there could be only a limited number of options open to us, varying between the radical extremes of handling all our traffic in Group vehicles, or handing it all to outside carriers; of completely decentralising all transport arrangements, or mounting a highly centralised operation. There were a few important questions which the study should answer — for example, how should traffic be allocated between the Group's own transport fleets and other carriers? Where should transport facilities be located ? How many vehicles of each size and type were needed? How should Group fleets be operated? How should the services of outside carriers, if they were needed, be bought?

The study would be aimed at answering the questions, at developing the more promising options, and at choosing between them.

5   Data collection

The questions could not themselves be answered until answers were found to many more questions about current practices, about the economics of transport operations, and about the commercial needs of Courtaulds' companies, etc. Not all of these questions could even be framed sensibly at the early stages of the study, but those which could made up a formidable list, from which a complex programme of interrelated tasks was derived.

Central to the whole project was the need to build up, and to manipulate, a reasonably accurate record of the sources, destinations, quantities, form, and costs of all Group companies' traffic.

Building the record was to be a protracted process, and one that had to be precisely adjusted to our needs. In a smaller scale study, the gathering of some information which later proves to be superfluous can be tolerated as the extra costs of data collection are small compared with the risk of inadequate records. In this case, however, the costs of collection were relatively large — the work of many busy people must not be disrupted merely to provide an assurance that our records would be plentiful. The survey was carefully planned to give us the necessary information in a form which would minimise the costs of providing it.

Visits were made to selected units, both to gather information from them to build up the record directly, and to define clearly the data which could be obtained reasonably economically. From those visits, a questionnaire was drawn up for circulation to each company, to establish the geography of its distribution network, the operation, cost and efficiency of the transport fleet available to each unit, its use and costs of outside carriers, and the organisation by which it planned, operated, and controlled its transport and distribution system.

Manipulating the record could also have been costly — details of monthly traffic movements on some 10,000 different routes were collected and analysed. We planned and wrote a suite of computer programmes to hold all the essential details of the traffic network, to give us the facility for rapidly sorting, extracting, and summarising the mass of otherwise indigestible data. Using this suite, for example, we developed a simple view of the network as movements along a few traffic lanes between and within nine major manufacturing and market areas. Each lane had reasonably stable characteristics and offered opportunities for coordinated traffic movements. This concept was to form one of the key features of practical policy in later operations.

6   Formulating the OR problems

Alongside the survey of traffic, a whole range of interrelated studies was carried out to provide a firm basis of established fact for future developments. A few examples may illustrate the problems tackled. Members of the team were assigned to

(a)   build up mathematical expressions to simulate the operation of available vehicle types throughout the network to assess costs and service capabilities with reasonable accuracy;

(b)   assess the economics and practicability of rationalising packages, unit loads, handling methods, and vehicle types, in cooperation with packaging and mechanical handling specialists;

(c)   estimate the notional profitability of fleet operations and the scope for economies by, for example, better routing and scheduling techniques;

(d)   investigate pricing structures and practices in the transport markets.

Some of the problems tackled are well known, in one form or another, in the OR trade, and techniques have been developed for providing near-optimal answers to them — for instance, the routing and scheduling of delivery vehicles, the location of transit depots, and the economic replacement of vehicles as they grow older. The studies drew upon the work of others in these areas — from papers in the journals, from internal reports, and by discussions with people inside and outside the Courtaulds Group. For the most part, the more highly developed techniques were useful in illuminating the structure of problems, and in suggesting the approach to be used rather than in providing answers. They often demanded more detailed information than we could obtain, or answered very specific questions which were different from those posed in our studies. The available techniques for vehicle scheduling, for instance, deal with the situation in which a fleet of loaded vehicles makes multiple deliveries from a single despatch point: our schedules not only involved many despatch points, but vehicles commonly collected goods and made deliveries on the same journey, changing the essential problem. The most useful techniques in this, as in other OR studies, were the most general — simple statistical analysis and elementary mathematical calculations.

7   Illustration

The use of these elementary techniques may be shown by outlining, in a simplified form, the argument of one of those interrelated studies. The study set out to calculate the economic balance between the use of company-owned vehicles and of outside carriers for a particular type of traffic — what proportion of the total traffic should we aim to carry in our own vehicles?

Two different reasons for using outside carriers were identified:

1   On some routes, total carriers' charges were less than the cost of operating a vehicle, generally because of the small amount of traffic, but length of journey, loading and unloading times, and the existence of return loads were all relevant. A straightforward but lengthy mathematical expression was developed to calculate the cost of operating a vehicle on any route, and carriers' charges for the same traffic were estimated from another expression derived, in turn, from a statistical analysis of rate scales and invoices. These expressions were used to compare costs of the alternatives on each route. In the particular traffic system studied, 10% of the total traffic would be handled by outside carriers on this cost comparison. (The value of developing a set of simple decision rules based on this analysis for use by traffic despatchers was also noted.)

2   The economic size of fleet also depended on the way demand varied through the year. In principle, at least, the first vehicle in a fleet could be used in the most profitable way, and vehicles could be added until the last one was just paying its way — until the costs of operating that last vehicle (including an element for return on capital) were equal to the alternative costs of using outside carriers. The relevant figures were the fixed annual cost of operating a vehicle (£456 p.a. per ton of capacity), the variable cost in daily operation (£0.80 per ton carried), and average carriers' charges for the same traffic (£4.60 per ton). The last ton of capacity should be operated on enough days of the year to break even, with number of days (d) being found from

$$456 + d\ 0.80 = d\ 4.60$$

so that

$$d = 120$$

With about 240 working days in the year, the vehicle would break even if fully utilised for six months, and a fleet should therefore be large enough to carry the median daily traffic in the year.* It should be supplemented by outside carriers in

---

*The **median** is the 'halfway point': the traffic level which is exceeded on precisely 50% of occasions.

peak periods, and would have some idle capacity in off-peak times.

From a study of the variation in that traffic through the year, which showed a peak about 25% above average, it was estimated that traffic handed to outside carriers for this reason would be about 7% of the total.

Taking 1 and 2 together, the work suggested that an upper limit to any growth of Group fleets in this area should be set at around 80—85% of traffic movements. Since only 50—60% of this particular traffic was being moved in our own vehicles, the practical value of this study was in encouraging a general policy of transferring traffic to our fleets.

8   Selecting solutions

Some of the studies resulted in numeric values of parameters, or clear, unequivocal statements of fact; others could only indicate areas for future work where the chances of profitable outcome were fairly good; and a few failed to produce any satisfactory answer at all. As the individual studies were completed, the analysis gave way to the more subjective tasks of interpreting the results, of simplifying the concepts, of projecting these ideas on to the Group as we knew it, and of designing tentative distribution systems which would both meet the newly established requirements and be robust enough to survive the inevitable knocking they would receive in the world outside. There was a close parallel with the design of any production system: the basic problem was to achieve an economic balance between production facilities, represented by vehicles, depots, and sub-contracted work, and the output requirements, which were, in this case, the traffic movements.

As the initial project deadline approached, some main features of appropriate distribution policy and practice became clear. The number, location, and interdependence of Group factories and warehouses, characteristic of a vertically integrated textile company, presented a unique problem and, therefore, a unique opportunity. There were 45 traffic lanes between and within the Group's nine major manufacturing and market areas. Each lane was made up of many individual traffic routes, and 14

lanes accounted for 80% of our traffic costs. Substantial economies with no overall loss of service standards could be obtained
by coordinated movements along all lanes, but along those 14 in
particular. Two complementary transport systems were designed
for that purpose — the one to carry traffic with an average
consignment size greater than half a ton, and the other for
smaller consignments. Both systems provided for the allocation
of traffic to the most appropriate size and type of Group vehicle,
or to other carriers, on the twin criteria of relative costs and
delivery service requirements. The 'bulk' system proposed a network of 100 heavy traffic routes, regularly serviced by Group
transport, and 800 other routes with a higher percentage of outside carriage. The 'smalls' system was more radical, and envisaged
a collection, trunking and delivery service which resembled a
typical large-scale parcels carrier's network rather than a conventional manufacturer's distribution system.

These systems were too large to be specified in detail within
the time limits. Even on some very rigorous assumptions about
the matching of traffic with appropriate vehicles, about capacity
utilisation and operating efficiencies, it was estimated that total
requirements would not be less than 1500 vehicles, either Group-
owned or bought in the form of capacity from other carriers,
and with a rather different mix of vehicle sizes and types from
the existing set up. It was recognised too that some vital features
of effective transport — the skills of individual managers and
despatchers, beneficent working relationships and practices
built up over a long period — could not be modelled in our
figures, but needed to be incorporated into the reality of an
efficient system. The systems were seen, therefore, as long-term
objectives — the outline statement of a transport plan which
could be improved in practice with progressively closer cooperation and coordination among units.

These, and other more detailed ideas for short-term developments, were assembled and presented to senior management by
the executives to whom the team reported.

9   Implementation

Not all the recommendations were accepted — in particular,
the team's ideas on the organisation which should be called into

being appeared too formal and rigid for the Group. Nevertheless, there was enough to enable practical development to go ahead in one of the more important and complex production and distribution centres — Lancashire.

A new phase of the work began — the longest, most difficult, but in many ways the most exciting and rewarding part of the OR man's trade — implementation (which is, of course, the only valid reason for pursuing an OR study). The work was no longer confined to a small study team, but involved, from the beginning, scores of operating managers and specialists responsible for the day-to-day administration and development of traffic and transport in the North West area. The OR analysts came out from behind their desks to combine their ideas with those of practical transport men and company divisional managers in an exercise that was dubbed the North West Transport Experiment. Vehicles were re-routed to give better utilisation; new commercial agreements were made with outside carriers; transport links were forged between Group units along the major traffic lanes; and coordination meetings were held, both to bring transport men together and to hack out new approaches within the overall traffic plan. New problems arose too — the pricing of transport services 'sold' within the Group proved particularly thorny.

After six months of the experiment, it was estimated that savings were running at the rate of rather more than £120,000 per annum, and there were other benefits which could not easily be quantified. Decisions were made to extend the approach more widely.

That work is still in progress; OR people are still involved, and there is still a long way to go to achieve the highly coordinated traffic network and transport systems envisaged. The OR role changed, of course, as we moved from the initial somewhat academic assessment of a problem perceived by senior managers, to the current commitment, working alongside middle and junior managers in their daily operations. The purpose of this chapter has been to describe that changing role. It is the view of one of the OR people involved, biased, maybe, and not sufficiently detached to place the whole project in its true perspective. Nevertheless, it is in many ways a typical example of an OR project and one which conveys the flavour of 'doing OR'.

4
Critical Path Methods

J B KIDD

1 Introduction

Major construction projects (of roads, airports, ships, etc.) typically comprise a large number of interrelated tasks involving a variety of different men and equipment. Since there may be millions of pounds at stake, it is worth spending time trying to schedule efficiently the various activities so as to reduce the time during which expensive items of machinery are tied up on site, and indeed to reduce or control the total completion time of the whole project.

In the late 1950's two systematic approaches were developed for this kind of coordination problem. They were named the **critical path method** (CPM) and the **project evaluation and review technique** (PERT); recently the general term **project network analysis** has been adopted. The technique is, in essence, a very simple one, and had been quite widely practised under different titles in many industrial situations. It is still used by the early practitioners — for example, by the CEGB in the maintenance and construction of power station equipment (see next chapter), by General Electric Company, by all the major civil engineering firms, and so on.

The method to be described is applicable to projects which satisfy the following conditions:

(a) The project consists of a well-defined collection of jobs. The completion of all these jobs marks the end of the project.

(b)   The jobs must follow a defined technological order, and it is specified which jobs must be completed before others can begin.

(c)   Subject to the above condition, the jobs can be started and stopped independently of each other.

We shall begin by analysing a situation in which the time necessary to carry out each job is assumed known with certainty and in which there are no resource constraints on the scheduling of jobs. Interest lies solely in determining the earliest completion time for the project, the earliest and latest times at which each job can be started and finished, the amount of leeway on each job, and so on. Later in the chapter, we shall explore ways of handling uncertainty about job times and resource limitations.

2   A simple example

A chemical manufacturer is interested in minimising the time taken to appraise the potential profitability of new products developed by the research division. The appraisal procedure is as follows. Salesmen are sent into the field for 14 days to investigate potential sales volumes. The plant manager then takes seven days to plan the necessary manufacturing facilities and the accountant takes a further four days to cost out this plan. Meanwhile, on the basis of the salesmen's reports, the sales manager takes three days to prepare a detailed schedule of likely selling prices. The cost and price data are then forwarded to the finance division, which takes 10 days to appraise the profitability of the venture.

Table 1   Data for the example

Job description	Job code letter	Duration (days)	Immediately preceding jobs	Starting node	Finishing node
Sales forecast	a	14	—	1	2
Unit pricing	b	3	a	2	4
Production schedule	c	7	a	2	3
Production costing	d	4	c	3	4
Budget preparation	e	10	b, d	4	5

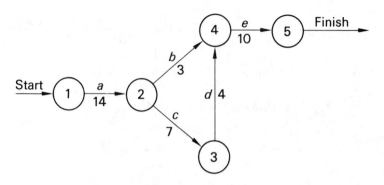

Figure 1. Activity network for the example

Table 1 lists the five jobs in this situation, with their expected duration and a note of the other jobs which must precede each job. In fact, it is sufficient to specify the jobs which *immediately* precede each job. For convenience, each job is given a code letter from *a* to *e*.

These jobs may be represented graphically in a **network** where each job corresponds to an **arrow** between two **nodes**, as shown in figure 1, with the job time noted below the arrow.* Each job is uniquely identified by its starting and finishing node, and each node corresponds to the starting or completion of one or more jobs. For convenience, the nodes have been numbered from 1 to 5. As a matter of good practice, the diagram should allow time to flow from left to right, so that arrows do not point backwards. Note how the network expresses the dependency between the jobs: after job *a* has been completed then *b* or *c* or both can begin, but *e* cannot begin until both *b* and *d* have been completed.

Before analysing this network, we shall introduce one additional job in order to illustrate the concept of a 'dummy

*There is an alternative method of drawing networks known as the **activity on the node** method, in which the nodes themselves represent jobs and the arrows define the technological sequencing of the jobs. This method will enable diagrams to be constructed with great ease as few if any 'dummies' (see later) have to be employed, but until recently computer programmes would not accept input in this form.

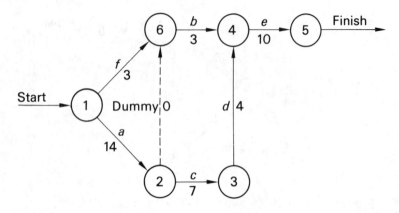

Figure 2. Revised activity network

activity'. Suppose the chemical firm wishes to survey competitors' selling prices before setting its own prices. This job can be undertaken in parallel with the survey of sales volume, but will take only three days and need not necessarily be completed before the production scheduling begins.

If the new job, labelled f, is incorporated in the network by allowing it to run in parallel with job a between nodes 1 and 2, then this implies that f must be completed before job c begins, which is incorrect. Moreover, two different jobs (a and f) are identified by the same start and finish nodes, which is undesirable. The problem is solved by introducing a new node 6 and a dummy activity which absorbs no time or other resource. The network is modified and the nodes relabelled as shown in figure 2.

3 Time analysis

There are many methods used to derive the essential data. Some methods are tabular, others rely on various annotations of the network diagram; all require simple calculations to find, for each job:

the earliest start time (ES)
the earliest finish time (EF)

the latest start time (LS)
the latest finish time (LF)

The following method annotates the network so that each activity shows the above calculated data, in addition to its brief description and its duration, according to the following convention:

Assume that the earliest time activity *a* can start is at time zero, then the earliest finish is in day 14. (In many computer-based methods it is possible to use calendar dates, rather than time periods.) The earliest start of both the dummy and job *c* must then be 14, since we assume that a new job may be begun immediately upon the completion of the preceding jobs. The earliest start of job *b* is 14, which is the *maximum* of 3 (the earliest finish of job *f*) and 14 (the earliest finish of the dummy). In this way we fix all activities at their earliest start time and complete all the ES, EF calculations. This is known as the **forward pass** through the network. This procedure yields the data above the activity lines in figure 3.

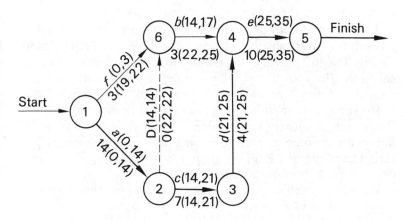

Figure 3. Time analysis

The forward pass shows that the whole project will take at least 35 days to complete, if all jobs are begun at their earliest start time. We now wish to calculate the latest time at which each job may be begun and still enable the project to be completed in 35 days. Evidently, if the latest finish for job e is 35 then the latest start is $35-10 = 25$, which in turn constitutes the latest finish for jobs b and d, and so on. This procedure is known as the **backward pass**. Note that when two or more jobs flow out from any node, as at node 2 in the example, then the latest finish time for the job leading into the node is the *minimum* of the two or more latest starts. Thus, the latest finish of job a is 14, which is the minimum of 22 (the LS on dummy) and 14 (the LS on job c). The LS, LF information is entered below the activity lines in figure 3.

These two sets of calculations complete the time analysis of the critical path method. Notice that certain of the jobs in figure 3 have their ES = LS and their EF = LF. This implies that if the duration of any of these jobs increases by as little as one time period, the EF and the LF will also increase, thereby causing succeeding jobs to be delayed. The coincidence of schedule times ES = LS and EF = LF along a continuous sequence of jobs defines the **critical path**. In our example the critical path (shown in heavy lines) passes through nodes 1, 2, 3, 4, 5 and comprises the jobs *a, c, d, e*. Consequently, if any of these four jobs is delayed in commencing, or takes longer than estimated, the project will exceed 35 days duration.

Jobs which do not lie along the critical path are called **sub-critical**; for these jobs there is some flexibility concerning their timing. The difference between the early and late start times is called the **float** for that job. Thus, job f has a float of $19 - 0 = 19$ days and job b has a float of $22 - 14$ days = 8 days.

However, a moment's reflection suggests that these two floats are not entirely independent of each other. The float of 8 days on job b only exists providing job f is completed by b's early start time of 14, and it disappears completely if job f is delayed until its latest start time.

We may, therefore, say that the **total float** for the chain of jobs f and b is 19 days and consists of two parts — an **independent float** of 11 days during which f may be delayed without affecting the ES of b, plus a **conditional float** of $19 - 11 = 8$ days which can be taken by either f or b, but not both.

The concept of float is important when attempting to schedule jobs to take account of the skills or resources needed to undertake the jobs (see later in this chapter). However, it can be a difficult task to extract the conditional and independent floats existing within real networks having long chains of jobs, which themselves may be interwoven.

4 Uncertainty of time estimates — PERT

The protagonists of PERT argue that it is impossible to be certain that a job will take exactly three days or six weeks or whatever duration is assumed in the critical path method. If the estimator knows his business then his estimate will usually be about right, but the job *may* be completed earlier or later; unexpected delays always occur somewhere. To cope with this, the PERT method calls for the estimation of the usual time (U) of each job and also an optimistic time (O) and a pessimistic time (P), chosen so that the actual time will fall outside the optimistic–pessimistic range only about once in every hundred jobs. These three estimates are used to calculate the following two parameters:*

$$\text{Mean job time} = \frac{O + 4U + P}{6}$$

$$\text{Variance of job time} = \left[\frac{(P - O)}{6}\right]^2$$

The critical path is calculated as before using mean job times, but then information about variances is used to calculate the likelihood of completing the project at different times. A detailed exposition of the proposed method is beyond the scope of the present book, but the following example will give the flavour of the approach.

Consider the project depicted in figure 4, where the pair of numbers on each activity line now correspond respectively to

*These formulae are based on the Beta distribution which is often recommended as a way of describing the probability distribution of times of a given job.

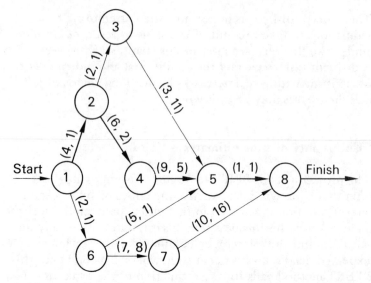

Figure 4. Example of PERT calculations with uncertainty

the mean time in days and the variance in 'days squared' of that activity. Suppose there were a penalty clause to be invoked, if the project exceeds 23 days' duration.

By calculation or inspection, it can be shown that the critical path is through nodes 1, 2, 4, 5, 8 and has a total mean duration of 4 + 6 + 9 + 1 = 20 days. Thus, there would appear to be no problem with the penalty clause. In fact, there would appear to be 3 days in hand.

But what of the information about variability of job durations? Providing there are a large number of jobs in the project, and providing the actual durations of the jobs are not too 'correlated' (i.e. affected in the same direction by weather or other common influences) then one can make an approximate calculation. We can assume that the actual time for any long chain of jobs will follow a normal distribution with mean equal to the total mean time for those jobs and variance equal to the sum of the individual variances of that chain of jobs.

In the present example, the mean time along the critical path is 20 days with a variance of 1 + 2 + 5 + 1 = 9. Now 23 days is $(23 - 20)/\sqrt{9} = 1$ standard deviation about the mean. We may calculate that the probability of completion before day 24 is 84%. Hence there is a 16% chance of incurring the penalty clause. But this is not all. There may be a chance of unusual delays along any sub-critical route. For example, the route through nodes 1, 6, 7, 8 has a total mean duration of $2 + 7 + 10 = 19$ days but a variance of $1 + 8 + 16 = 25$. Now 23 days is $(23 - 19)/\sqrt{25} = 0.8$ standard deviations about the mean value, so there is only a 78% chance of completing this route within 23 days. The chance of completing both routes in 23 days is given by the product of their probabilities, i.e. $0.84 \times 0.78 = 0.65$. There is thus a 35% chance of failing to meet the deadline because of delays on one of these two routes. In general, other routes should also be investigated but, in this example, they have a reasonable degree of float and the probability of their causing trouble is slight.

In practice, people seem to underestimate the likelihood of 'extreme' outcomes: actual job times tend to fall outside the optimistic—pessimistic range perhaps one third of the time rather than about 1% of the time.[2] The project variances and consequently the risks are thus underestimated. It is difficult to know how to correct for this, since each estimator varies in his degree of conservatism. One way is to 'audit' estimates that have been made to determine whether particular individuals are biased towards optimism or pessimism. In the present example it is conceivable that modifications for this factor would increase the chance of not meeting the 23-day deadline to, say, 50%.

By undertaking such analyses one can indicate to management the problems which are inherent in the project. But these results are not obtained cheaply — three estimates are required on each activity in order to calculate mean times and variances, and a full combinatorial analysis has to be undertaken (with conditional probabilities, if independence of delays cannot be assumed). All this takes time and money. If the project is important this detail could be mandatory, otherwise a 'simple' critical path study should be the limit of the complexity. Alternatively, one might use stochastic programming or simulation techniques, as described in Chapters 8 and 15. In any event, delays are important to everyone concerned, and it is necessary to have some way of taking them into account. The next chapter provides some further illustration and discussion of this point.

5   Concluding remarks

The methods so far described enable one to schedule jobs so as to minimise the expected completion time of the whole project, but no account has been taken of the resources required or the cost of the project. A manager might legitimately ask, for example, whether it is possible to schedule jobs so as not to exceed at any time the availability of mechanics, welders or electricians, and whether it is worth paying overtime wages to speed up certain jobs in order to avoid lateness penalties. Unfortunately, no simple technique is available for answering such questions. In simple situations **Gantt charts** (bar charts) can be useful for resource scheduling and monitoring progress. Where numerous resources are involved, it may be appropriate to employ one of the increasing number of computer packages which use **heuristic** scheduling rules, i.e. rules which are based on what seem to be good approaches, but which cannot be fully justified mathematically. One such programme is used by the CEGB as described in the next chapter.

As with many OR models, an important pay-off from using critical path techniques often comes, not from the detailed job schedules which result, but from the qualitative insights into which times, resources and jobs are likely to be critical. In the initial phase of drawing a network, various revised methods of tackling unusual jobs come to light and are incorporated into the diagram. If overall project completion time is unsatisfactory then it may be possible to speed up certain jobs, to omit other jobs or to alter the logic of the network by revising the technological order of jobs. It must be appreciated also that unexpected developments may occur 'on site' which take some time to be reflected in the control room charts, and which necessitate revising the calculations. Nevertheless, as remarked at the beginning of this chapter, most large companies find it worthwhile to use the technique and the next chapter describes one such application.

References and further reading

1   Kelley J. E., 'Critical path planning and scheduling: mathematical basis', *Operations Research*, vol. 9, May 1961.

2   Kidd J. B., 'Measurement of bias in project estimates', *R and D Management*, October 1975.

3   Miller R. W., *Schedule, Cost and Profit Control with PERT*, McGraw-Hill 1963.

4   Wiest J. D. and Levy F. K., *A Management Guide to PERT/CPM*, Prentice Hall 1969.

Exercises

1   Show how the first example in the chapter (section 2) would be represented using the 'activity on the node' method

2   The following table gives details of 20 activities which comprise a project where some must be completed before others can start.

    (a)   Draw a network diagram for this project.
    (b)   Calculate the critical path and explain its significance.
What is the minimum completion time for the whole project?

Activity	Duration (days)	Activities which must precede it
A	5	—
B	9	—
C	4	—
D	4	A
E	3	A
F	10	B
G	6	D
H	12	D
I	10	F, G
J	3	C
K	4	C
L	5	J
M	5	J
N	8	K, L
O	18	M, N
P	3	H, I, O
Q	6	P
R	13	P
S	5	Q
T	7	R, S

(c)   Calculate the earliest and latest start time for activity M.

(d)   If time on activity F were cut to 6 days, how much sooner would the project be finished?

(e)   If time on job K were lengthened to 9 days, by how much would the whole project be delayed?

3   Consider the following table of data relating to a certain project.

Activity	Immediate precedent(s)	Estimates of activity time (days): Optimistic	Usual	Pessimistic
A	—	0.7	1.0	1.3
B	A	3.8	5.6	9.8
C	A	5.2	7.6	12.4
D	B	2.1	2.7	5.1
E	B	2.0	6.8	12.8
F	C, D	0.7	3.4	3.7
G	E, F	0.7	1.0	1.3

(a)   Construct the activity network for this situation.

(b)   Calculate the critical path using the usual time estimates. Calculate earliest and latest start and finish times for each activity. How much float is there on non-critical activities?

(c)   How confident would you be that the whole project would be completed in 15 days?

4   A jobbing contractor wins a contract to build concurrently five petrol stations along a motorway. He has to complete all

Activity description	Activity name	Immediate precedents	Mean time (days)	Variance (days^2)
Open up site	A	—	3	1
Civ. eng. work	B	A	15	3
Mech. eng. work	C	A	10	2
Mech. eng. work (in detail)	D	C	4	1
Instrumentation	E	D	4	1
Lay electrical circuits	F	C	4	1
Finish civ. eng. work	G	B, F	5	1
Run-up, check, close site	H	E, G	7	1

five in 35 days. Each project has the following characteristics.
(Assume no common resource constraints.)

(a) Could he complete a single project in 35 days?
(b) What are his chances of completing all five projects on
time? (Hint: If p is the probability of success in a certain
experiment, and if the experiment is repeated n times, then
the (joint) probability of success in all n experiments is p^n.)
(c) What would be the effect of his losing control over these
projects as indicated by (i) an increase in the mean job times;
(ii) an increase in the variance of job times?

5

Maintenance Planning in the CEGB

N A SIMPSON

1 Introduction

Project network analysis has evolved in various forms over the last 15 years. It has been adapted and applied successfully by many different industries to a variety of projects. Nevertheless, the results achieved have at times been disappointing. Considerable time and effort have therefore been spent in attempting to improve the detailed methods of analysis, with a view to achieving the 'optimal' solution. These attempts have often resulted in negligible benefits. Under controlled laboratory conditions these 'improved' techniques would probably be more valuable. However, the normal industrial environment is uncertain and involves the complex interaction of groups of individuals. Required data are seldom fully available, and in any case are changing.

The Central Electricity Generating Board (CEGB) has been involved in the development of project network analysis from the beginning. Because it has a large annual maintenance and construction programme, and because this kind of work is characterised by uncertainty, interaction and change, the CEGB has placed particular emphasis on the development of techniques for assisting in the managerial control of these programmes.

The planning of a major plant shutdown in the CEGB involves regional and national liaison to ensure compatibility of work programmes with contractors and manufacturers resources. The lost production caused by the shutdown also has to be assessed against the total demand for electricity that may have to be met. As electricity cannot be effectively stored in large quantities, the CEGB has to have an installed capacity capable of meeting the maximum demand which occurs in the winter. Excess plant capacity, at this time, is planned to a minimum level consistent with an acceptable risk. The annual maintenance repair programme requiring plant shutdown is therefore constrained to the summer period of low demand. Within the resource constraints, the plant shutdowns are scheduled to minimise the cost of meeting the demand. The plant with low production cost must operate for the maximum period between the statutory inspection limits specified by the insurance certificates.

The planning process increases in detail over a three-year period. The only firm information available at the start of this cycle is that the unit will have to be shut down at some time in the future. It is therefore not surprising that intentions change over this period and final plans may differ significantly from the original ones. This planning cycle is a continuous process so that at any one time plans for different plant shutdowns will be in various stages of preparation. In addition, more than one major plant shutdown may occur on the same site, thus increasing the magnitude of the problem.

The problems that occur with the shutdown maintenance on the low production cost plant are comparable with those to be found in many other industries where there are competing work priorities for the operating plant, and the staff involved, including contractors, work complex multiple shift patterns.

2   The approach used

The following example describes a statutory overhaul on a 120 megawatt turbine generator/boiler unit in the Midlands Region of the Central Electricity Generating Board. The method used accepted the uncertainty of the basic data and attempted to overcome this by using a system that could respond rapidly to known changes of work content and duration, thereby providing responsive management control of the project. The

programme data were set up and operated by the line management responsible for the project. It was therefore possible for
them to use their judgment in modifying the network structures
and activity durations. Adjustments could be made for the
probable variance of time estimates of individual jobs and for
the risk of new work areas occurring.

A continuous surveillance and updating procedure was
adopted with new schedules being processed once per week and
within a 36 hour turnround. If necessary, further schedules
could have been processed as required. This allowed frequent
changes to be made to the data as necessary. All updating information was input via a computer terminal as it became available
and was then stored until a new schedule needed to be processed.

The computer programme used was the SMART 2 programme
(Scheduling Manpower And Resources Techniques) which has
recently been evolved by the CEGB. The programme uses the
serial scheduling method whereby critical jobs are scheduled
first and the less critical jobs are initiated as resources are freed.
Processing time is relatively short, and resource scheduling can
be controlled by the user.

3   Plan preparation

In order to provide the extent of flexibility required, it was
necessary to design carefully the details of the work programmes.

Basic data modules were developed which contained standard
networks for the complete overhaul of particular plant items.
These modules were then linked together by dummy activities to
form **sub-networks** of whole plant areas. Finally, **operational
networks** were obtained by joining together the sub-networks.
The total network contained ten sub-networks and totalled 1600
activities.

The method proved to be simple and effective. Checks on
data validity were carried out at each stage of building up the
operational networks. In order to allow clerical staff to load the
computer input directly from the networks, the original
networks were modified and redrawn. The effort involved in
preparing the networks and inputting data was approximately 55
engineer man-days and 20 clerical man-days.

Normal resource scheduling methods can produce schedules that are impractical at the working level. The present system overcomes this by using **working calendars** against which the activities are scheduled. For example, an activity involving radiographic work would be constrained to periods when a minium of other work in progress would be expected (often at night). Key events were entered to assist in the selection of management reports. Update reports were received on a regular basis and daily reporting times were given to all contractors. Where necessary, spot checks were made on critical items. These frequencies were revised near the end of the shutdown when only weekly reports were required. In practice, variations in reporting frequency were found to be acceptable depending on the type of work involved and its importance. It was found that daily reporting could result in an unmanageable amount of information. Usually, the update information averaged about 150

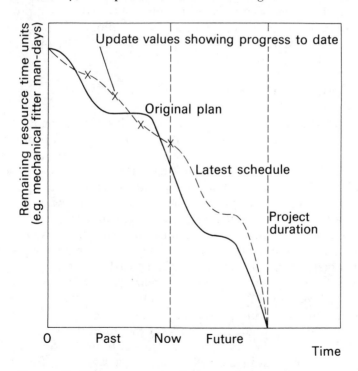

Figure 1. Progress evaluation

activities per week. The pattern was typical of an overhaul in that extensive alterations to work content were made after two to three weeks when the work assessment was completed. After this time, modifications to the plan were steady for the central part of the work programme, increasing towards the end as plant was commissioned and finally tailing off.

Increases in the remaining work, increased work content of completed activities or a reduced work rate can result in the remaining float of a resource schedule being progressively absorbed without the effect being obvious from the update schedule. These changes may be undetected until a key date is violated. It may then be too late to take corrective action to recover the situation.

To prevent this, data were extracted to show the used and remaining resource time units required compared with the original schedule. A typical form of the presentation is shown in figure 1; in this case the rate of completion to date is approximately on programme, whereas the remaining work programme requires considerably more resources than originally planned.

4   Progress and problems

The original plan, based on a time analysis assuming 24 hour continuous working, envisaged that the boiler would return to service on 5 September. However, the resulting resource schedule based on previously agreed working patterns gave a realistically achievable date of 20 October. The senior station management were consulted and, following negotiation, the contractor's working pattern on critical activities were adjusted. At the same time a detailed study of the resource usage histograms made it possible to readjust the work programme, thus relieving potential overloads on station resources. The revised resource schedules gave a return-to-service date of 29 September.

The beginning of the plant shutdown, when all engineering inspections are in progress, is the period when maximum change occurs. In the present case, the total slip up to this stage consisted of 11 days because the reheater boiler section was blocked with dust in the boiler rear gas passage and a further three days because insufficient resources had been allocated to certain boiler work. These resources had been committed to work being carried out on another section of the plant. This slip to the programme was irretrievable and 13 October was adopted as the revised target date for return to service.

Work then progressed for a number of weeks with the required rate of completion being maintained and no major problems arose. The next significant step was the boiler hydraulic test. Technical problems associated with completing the filling of the boiler with water and a subsequent boiler tube leak delayed the completion of the boiler hydraulic test by a further four days. The work programme was then in its final stages and the final content of jobs with highly variable work content was becoming known. During this period it became apparent that brickwork repairs were behind programme, and it was estimated that a further eight days of in-line work would be required. A review of the resource schedules at this time resulted in revised working patterns being adopted by a contractor on critical work which maintained the revised end date. A further delay of two days then occurred owing to incorrect refractory material being initially supplied. Finally, delays of four days occured because of technical problems during the setting of boiler safety valves. The unit was eventually synchronised on 31 October.

Delays generally fall into two classes, namely, those caused by technical problems and those caused by increased work content. Moreover, work content can progressively change as work progresses, e.g. boiler brickwork and refractory repairs. These latter are perhaps the most difficult to forecast and control, and it requires a rapid response system to cope effectively with possible changes in resource demand patterns.

The degree to which actual work content may vary from that planned is mainly dependent on the extent of the contingencies allowed for and the type of work involved. To some extent, variations can be reduced by increasing the level of work definition and measurement. Moreover, the original plan is often a balance between a forecast of the work expected to be found and a target that is a statement of intent. A work programme that is based on achieving a minimal overall duration theoretically has a lower chance of success than one that has extensive contingencies built in. However, complex motivational factors are involved which could considerably reduce the chance of success in achieving the latter and could result in unacceptably long durations.

5   Subsequent work

Two main actions have been initiated as a result of the findings during the system trial. These are:

1   A thorough investigation into boiler cleaning work with particular emphasis on:
(a)   improved estimates of work content,
(b)   assessing the resources required,
(c)   optimum methods of working.

2   Improved methods for speeding up the feedback of information on additional work found during the progress of work.

The repair programme was relatively standard and had been carried out before on other units. These previous repairs had used the normal organisational controls and the standard resource scheduling system that existed. A considerable amount of sound work measurement data therefore existed and this contributed to the level of control achieved.

The detailed resource schedules were obtained after the shutdown had started. These showed considerable resource overloads. However, further corrective managerial action was limited as work had already been re-allocated. Ideally, the schedules would have been produced some months before the contracts were placed so that an optimum programme could have been obtained. This was disrupted by the transfer to the new planning system. Nevertheless, significant progress has been made towards a flexible and responsive system which provides an adaptive control mechanism to assist in the management of work programmes.

6

Transportation and Network Problems

S C LITTLECHILD

1   The nature of the transportation problem

Many companies produce goods in a relatively small number
of factories and ship these to a number of warehouses throughout the country. The goods are then distributed from the warehouses to a large number of retailers. In the case of the major
oil companies one is talking about refineries, depots and garages.
Similar situations arise on the purchasing side — for example, the
West Midlands Gas Board used to purchase coal from a variety
of collieries and transport it to their manufacturing plants.
   The companies concerned have to answer the following kinds
of question:

1   What is the best location for each factory/refinery/
warehouse/depot/gas plant?
2   What is the best level of production/purchase at each
factory/refinery/colliery?
3   Which factory/refinery/colliery should supply which
warehouse/depot/gas plant?

Obviously, these questions are interrelated, and if one were
starting a business from scratch, they would need to be
answered virtually simultaneously. However, an established
business will already have factories located in certain places,
which it would be a major operation to re-locate. The location
of the suppliers and customers is largely out of the hands of the

business. Levels of production may be adjusted more easily, but there may be capacity limitations, existing commitments, or specialisation of staff or equipment, for example. Perhaps the most readily adjustable operations concern the distribution system.

It is therefore possible to pose the questions in the following manner.

1   Given the location of the factories/depots/suppliers/ customers, and also given the volumes of production and requirements at these places, what is the best transportation or distribution pattern for the products in question?
2   In the light of the answer to question 1, what adjustments in levels of production are indicated?
3   In the light of the answers to questions 1 and 2, should the location of the company's premises be reconsidered?

This chapter will be almost entirely concerned with the first of these questions (i.e. the pattern of distribution) but it will be seen that the approach used throws a great deal of light on the second question (i.e. levels of production). At the end of the chapter we refer briefly to techniques for solving the plant location problem.

We shall not be concerned here with the mode of transportation (e.g. whether to ship by road or rail, whether to operate one's own fleet of lorries or buy outside) but rather with the pattern of distribution. More precisely, given a set of *origins* with specified product *availabilities* at each, given a set of *destinations* with specified *requirements* at each, and given the *per unit cost* of transporting products from each origin to each destination, what is the cheapest feasible pattern of shipments from origins to destinations? This problem is known as the **standard transportation problem.** In the last section of the chapter we shall show how the transportation problem is one of a more general class of **network** problems, and in Chapter 8 we shall show that it is also a simple type of **linear programme.** It will be seen that a wide variety of problems, which do not involve physical transportation, can nevertheless be formulated and solved as standard transportation problems.

2   The necessity for computer solution techniques

It may be thought that the standard transportation problem could be solved by hand, using a bit of common sense. It is indeed quite straightforward to enumerate and compare half a dozen possible distribution patterns. But bear in mind that if there are 10 depots and 20 retailers, then a feasible pattern of distribution is going to involve at least 20 shipments (one for each retailer) and there are 10 ways of choosing each shipment, so the number of possible combinations is of the order of 10^{20}. Suppose 99% of these alternatives could be immediately discarded as inefficient. Even if each remaining pattern could be evaluated in one second, it would still take over thirty thousand million man-years to complete the job. This means that if the cheapest possible solution is to be found, not only will a computer have to be used but also some more efficient method will have to be used than simply enumerating and comparing each alternative.

One may ask whether the best solution obtained by computer will be significantly better than that calculated by an experienced person. It may be only a few percentage points cheaper, but if the total distribution cost is of the order of millions of pounds per year, then the savings are likely to be of the order of tens of thousands of pounds per year. For example, 10 years ago the West Midlands Gas Board was able to save about 1% on its annual coal transportation costs of some £2½ million (see exercise 1 at the end of this chapter). The National Coal Board reports savings of 6% on the cost of transporting coal from 25 sources to nine washeries, and incidental benefits of the same magnitude from meeting sulphur restrictions which had not been achieved before. The large oil companies are believed to have obtained even more considerable savings, often up to 15% of relevant distribution costs.

3   An example

Methods for solving the standard transportation problem can best be discussed in terms of a simple numerical example.

Table 1   Capacities and requirements

Factory	Capacity	Warehouse	Requirement
Manchester	20 units	Manchester	11
Birmingham	10 units	Coventry	13
London	25 units	Birmingham	17
		Cardiff	14
Total supply	55	Total demand	55

Table 2   Transportation costs (£ per unit)

From:	To: Manchester	Coventry	Birmingham	Cardiff
Manchester	1	6	3	6
Birmingham	7	3	1	6
London	9	4	5	4

Suppose a company has factories at Manchester, Birmingham and London, and warehouses at Manchester, Coventry, Birmingham and Cardiff. For the coming planning period the factories and warehouses have the capacities and requirements set out in table 1. (We shall show later that there is no difficulty in handling situations where total requirements are not equal to total capacity.) Per unit transportation costs, by the cheapest mode of transport currently available, are given in table 2. What pattern of shipments will satisfy the requirements at minimum cost?

4   Laying out the problem

It is convenient to set out the basic information in a simple table — called a **transportation tableau** — as shown in figure 1. There is one row for each origin (factory) and one row for each destination (warehouse), consequently there is one **cell** for each possible shipment of goods. Capacities and requirements, as taken from table 1, are noted on the border of the tableau. In each cell, the number in the top left-hand corner indicates the

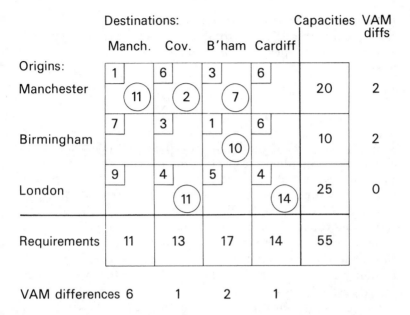

Figure 1. Transportation tableau with solution obtained by 'least-cost first' rule

unit cost of that shipment, as taken from table 2. (If for any reason it is impossible to ship along certain routes then, for the purpose of the present approach, a finite but very large cost is attributed to that cell; see for example exercise 2 at the end of this chapter.) The 'VAM differences' should be ignored until section 6.

Inside each cell we shall put the number of tons to be shipped along that route. A **feasible solution** is a set of entries which satisfies two conditions:

1   the entries must be non-negative, since (in this problem) negative shipments are not acceptable;

2   the entries must sum along each row to the capacity available at that factory, and down each column to the requirement of that warehouse.

The total transportation cost of any solution is obtained by multiplying each entry by the corresponding unit cost and summing overall entries. The object is to find the feasible solution(s) with the lowest total cost; this is called the **optimal solution** (strictly speaking, *an* optimal solution since it may not be unique).

5 'Least-cost first' rule

With a small problem like this it is possible to obtain a reasonable solution simply by inspecting the tableau. One could use the simple **least-cost first** rule of thumb: put as much as possible in the cell with lowest unit cost, then in the cell with second lowest cost, and so on. (In the case of a tie, arbitrarily pick one of the tied cells.) Thus, one would begin by shipping 11 units from factory to warehouse in Manchester, 10 units from factory to warehouse in Birmingham, 7 units from Manchester to Birmingham, and so on, to yield the solution already shown in figure 1, which has a total cost of £154.

One difficulty with this rule is that it does not take into account the implications of each choice; it does not 'look ahead'. In the simple example shown in figure 2 it would lead to shipments from A to C and from B to D, at a total cost of £1 + £10 = £11. However, a much cheaper solution is to avoid

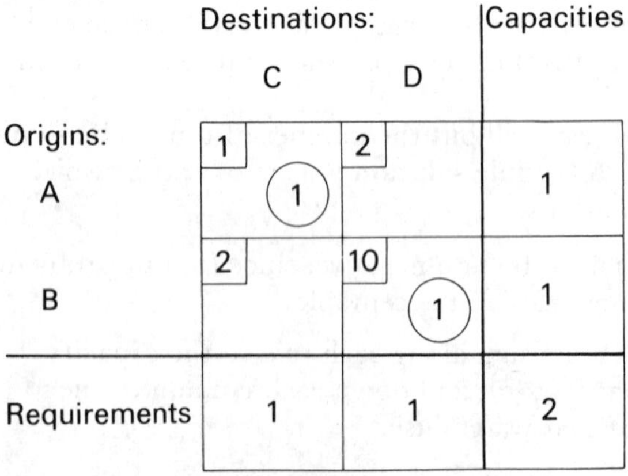

Figure 2. Example of failure of the 'least-cost first' rule

the least-cost cell AC altogether and ship one unit from A to D and one from B to C, for a total cost of £2 + £2 = £4.

6   Vogel's approximation method

A procedure which to some extent gets round this difficulty is **Vogel's approximation method** (VAM) which 'looks ahead' one step by considering the consequence of *not* choosing the best cell in each row and column. It therefore enables one to choose the cell which it is important not to miss. The method is quite simple.

1   Jot down the difference between the lowest and second lowest cost in each row.
2   Repeat for each column.
3   Identify the row or column with greatest difference (resolving ties arbitrarily).
4   Identify the cell in the chosen row or column which has the lowest cost.
5   Put as much as possible in the chosen cell.
6   Repeat the procedure, excluding the row or column which is now satisfied.
7   Continue until the entire amount is transported.

As with the least-cost first rule, one row or column is deleted at each step, so the maximum number of steps is the sum of the number of rows and columns.

VAM may be illustrated on our example. In figure 1 the VAM differences have been calculated and noted alongside each row and column. Since the greatest difference is 6, and the lowest cost in that column is 1, ship as much as possible from the Manchester factory to the Manchester warehouse, namely 11 units. (The factory has capacity for 20 units but the warehouse requires only 11 units.)

The calculations are repeated in figure 3, ignoring the Manchester warehouse (first column). The greatest difference is 3 and the lowest cost in that row is 3, hence ship 9 from Manchester to Birmingham, thereby exhausting capacity at the Manchester factory (first row). It may be verified that after four

Destinations:				Capacities	VAM diffs
Manch.	Cov.	B'ham	Cardiff		

Origins:	Manch.	Cov.	B'ham	Cardiff	Capacities	VAM diffs
Manchester	1 (11)	6	3 (9)	6	20	3
Birmingham	7	3	1	6	10	2
London	9	4	5	4	25	0
Requirements	11	13	17	14	55	
VAM differences −	1	2	1			

Figure 3. VAM method in process

more steps the solution shown in figure 4 is obtained. This has a total cost of £152.

7   Optimality and sensitivity analysis

VAM will generally yield a good solution; in the present example it saves just over 1% on the total cost of the previous solution. Is this the lowest cost solution available? If not, how can a better solution be found? As it happens, it is the optimal solution, but VAM itself cannot tell us this, nor can it locate any improvements if the solution it finds is not optimal.

Both VAM and the 'least-cost-first' rule are examples of **algorithms** — that is, sets of rules for finding solutions to specified problems — but they cannot guarantee to find the optimal solution. Algorithms have been developed for com-

Destinations:	Manch.	Cov.	B'ham	Cardiff	Capacities
Origins: Manchester	1 ⑪	6	3 ⑨	6	20
Birmingham	7	3 ②	1 ⑧	6	10
London	9	4 ⑪	5	4 ⑭	25
Requirements	11	13	17	14	53

Figure 4. VAM solution

pletely solving the transportation problem, which are not difficult to understand but are somewhat lengthy to describe and, indeed, time-consuming to work through by hand. However, we can illustrate the method using the present example.

Instead of shipping from Manchester to Birmingham and also from Birmingham to Coventry, would it perhaps be cheaper to ship direct from Manchester to Coventry? If this is done, it can be seen from figure 4 that in order to balance capacities and requirements it will also be necessary to increase the shipment from the Birmingham factory to the Birmingham warehouse. It can easily be verified that for every unit thus rearranged the net increase in total transport cost is £6 − £3 − £3 + £1 = £1, so the proposed modification is not worthwhile.

In the present example it is not too difficult to check out all possible changes to see if the VAM solution can be improved. (In fact, it is the optimal solution.) In a real problem of any size this would be quite impracticable. Fortunately, a procedure has been developed, known as the **row-column sum** or **stepping-stone**

method, which systematically checks whether any new shipments can profitably be introduced, calculates what compensating changes need to be made to existing shipments, and
repeats these checks and adjustments until the cheapest solution
is obtained. These repeated adjustments are known as iterations.

A second advantage of the stepping-stone method is that it
makes use of **shadow prices**, which reflect the change in total
transport cost induced by changes in capacities and requirements. We shall encounter shadow prices again when studying
linear programming (Chapter 8), and the reader may well have
met them when studying economics. Their immediate significance is that they allow us to carry out **sensitivity analysis**. We
may wish to know how sensitive is the optimal solution to
changes in costs, whether it is worth expanding factory
capacities or adjusting warehouse requirements, etc. For
example, answers can easily be provided to the following
questions:

> If unit transportation cost from London to Manchester were
> reduced from £9 to zero, would it be worth shipping along
> that route?
>
> If the unit cost of shipping from Manchester to Cardiff fell
> by £1, would Manchester become a viable alternative to
> London as a source for the Cardiff warehouse?
>
> At which factory should capacity be expanded in order to
> most reduce total transportation costs?
>
> What adjustment of warehouse requirements will most reduce
> total transportation costs?
>
> Is it ever possible to increase total units shipped and simul-
> taneously *decrease* total transportation cost?

The reader may like to attempt to answer these questions
himself.

Of course, in all this sensitivity analysis one would need to
take into account also the comparative investment and production costs of extending capacity at the different premises as well
as a variety of other less easily quantified considerations. Moreover, these shadow prices have the drawback that they refer only
to the first few units of extra capacity. For this reason, many

companies do not utilise this information. However, many other users, particularly national planners, find that the shadow prices at least draw attention to crucial bottlenecks and suggest likely areas for further investigation.

8   Further applications of the standard transportation model

The model just described is as applicable to profit maximisation as to cost minimisation situations. It can handle situations where origin availabilities and destination requirements are in the form of upper and lower bounds, rather than exact requirements, and where total capacity does not equal total demand. This is done by simply introducing 'dummy' activities with zero cost corresponding to spare capacity or unsatisfied demand. Upper and lower bounds can also be imposed on individual shipments without too much difficulty. Unit costs which *increase* with the amount shipped, rather than stay constant, can easily be incorporated. Unit costs which *decrease* with volume (e.g. as a result of quantity discounts or internal economies of scale) present certain difficulties beyond the scope of the present book (see also section 9 of Chapter 8).

Various problems which appear to be quite different from the standard transportation problem (because they involve no notion of physical movement) in fact have an identical structure, and may therefore be solved by the same technique.

Suppose a company has a number of factories or production lines which are each capable of producing a number of different products. The total capacity of each factory, the total demand for each product, and the unit cost of manufacturing each product at each factory are specified. The problem is formally identical to the standard transportation problem (with the different products in place of warehouses). This idea is incorporated in the model of a US automobile company described in the next chapter.

Or again, suppose a firm purchases raw materials at prices which vary month by month. Then it has to choose whether to produce to meet demand in each month or instead to produce in advance and hold inventory. This can be thought of as a transportation problem in which the origins and destinations correspond to different months of the year, and finished products or raw materials may be 'transported' from the month of production to the month of use at a specified inventory holding cost. An example is given in exercise 3 at the end of this chapter.

Now consider the problem of allocating salesmen to territories, where estimates can be made of the degree of success which each salesman is likely to have in each territory. Alternatively, consider the problem faced by the National Coal Board in allocating different machines to different coal faces in the light of data on machine efficiencies under different circumstances. If a different salesman/machine is best for each territory/coal face, then there is no problem, but in general things will not be this simple. These problems may be thought of as transportation problems with salesmen/machines as 'origins' and territories/coal faces as 'destinations'. There is a supply of one unit at each origin and a requirement of one unit at each destination. Unit costs are measured in terms of relative efficiencies. This special case of the transportation problem is known as the **assignment problem,** and even simpler techniques are available for solving such problems. The University of California is reported to use a student-professor-classroom assignment model, while the Office of Civilian Manpower Management of the US Navy has developed a sophisticated 'multi-objective multi-attribute planning model' for assignment of personnel.

9   Network flow models

Instead of representing transportation problems in tableau form, we could, alternatively, represent them as **networks,** with nodes corresponding to origins and destinations, and arcs corresponding to potential shipments. The example problem is shown in figure 5. Unit costs are shown in a small square on each arc (for a few arcs only). The problem is to choose flows on the arcs so as to minimise total costs subject to the condition that 'what goes in must come out' at each node.

Formulating the transportation problem in this way suggests that it is only one of a general class of network problems.

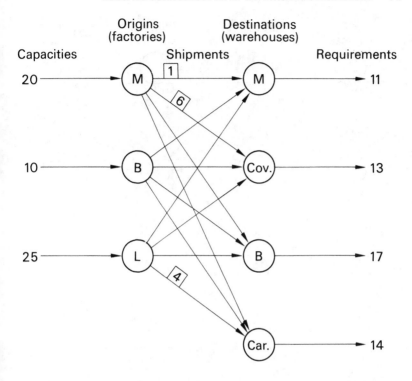

Figure 5. Network representation of transportation example

Another type is a **trans-shipment model** in which commodities are shipped through one or more intermediate nodes. For example, the major oil companies have to plan the shipment of oil from various foreign sources through various refineries and regional depots to individual garages. This problem could be represented as in figure 6. A similar model is used by Nabisco Inc. for scheduling production and distribution of their 'cookies' from factories to regional warehouses and then to local distribution facilities. The automobile example described in the next chapter is also presented in this way.

Inventory maintenance models are also of trans-shipment type. Here the 'origins' are purchases or production, at different dates, the ultimate 'destinations' are sales or usages, and the intermediate nodes represent inventory, as in figure 7. An

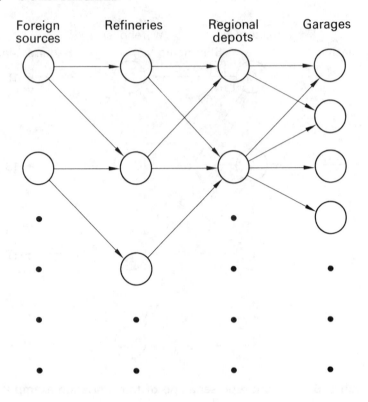

Figure 6. Trans-shipment model of an oil company

example is the New Mexico cotton-ginning problem referred to in the next chapter. It is possible to extend these models to incorporate hierarchies of national, regional, area and plant stores. The problem of hiring and firing personnel in the presence of strong seasonal demand swings can be represented in a similar way.

The problem of finding the *shortest route* through a network of towns from, say, Birmingham to Edinburgh can be thought of as a trans-shipment problem with only one origin and one destination. (The 'cost' is measured in miles.) Similarly, the critical path method described in Chapter 3 involves the calculation of the *longest route* in a network (where the 'cost' is measured in time).

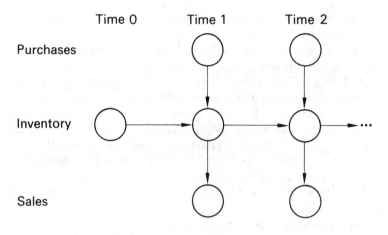

Figure 7. Inventory maintenance trans-shipment model

10   Fixed charge and generalized network models

Hitherto, we have assumed that total costs on any arc are proportional to volume shipped along that arc (i.e. there is simply a constant unit cost). However, in many cases there is also a **fixed charge** which is incurred if there is any flow at all, but which is independent of the volume of flow.

Plant location problems are of this kind — for example, the location of offshore oil drilling platforms and the assignment of wells to platforms; a model of this kind is reported to have been designed by the Soviet Union. Another example is the location of waste disposal collection centres in large cities, to which trucks from local collection areas bring refuse, to be subsequently transported to main dumps.

Notice that, once a set of plant locations has been chosen, the remaining problem, called a **sub-problems**, is of normal transportation or trans-shipment type. One might solve very small location problems by enumerating all possible plant location patterns and solving the associated transportation sub-problem for each. However, with as few as 10 prospective sites this would entail the solution of more than a million transportation problems. More sophisticated techniques are required; this is an area where significant computational advances are currently being made.

We have hitherto assumed that flow is not changed as it passes along an arc, but just as electric power deteriorates when transmitted over long distance, so inventories may be subject to pilferage or wastage, and money borrowed or invested depreciates or appreciates by the amount of the interest charge. Networks which include arcs of this character are called **generalised networks**. An example is a **generalised assignment model** developed for the US Office of Naval Research to minimise transportation and overhaul costs at naval shipyards.

Algorithms are available for solving all the various types of transportation and network flow models discussed above, but the details will not be of much interest to the general reader. What is important to note, as the following chapter emphasises, is that the development of extremely efficient algorithms has brought to the aid of the manager the rapid computer solution of an increasing number and variety of very large-scale allocation problems.

References and further reading

1   Charnes A. and Cooper W. W., *Management Models and Industrial Application of Linear Programming* (2 vols), Wiley 1961.

2   Ford L. R. and Fulkerson D. R., *Flows in Networks*, Princeton University Press 1962.

3   Wagner H. M., *Principles of Operations Research*, Prentice Hall 1969.

Exercises

1   Draw up the transportation tableau of the following problem:

Origin	Availability	Destination	Requirement
1	22	1	30
2	41	2	45
3	27	3	15
4	10		
	100		90

Unit transportation costs in £
Destination:

		1	2	3
Origin:	1	3	1	4
	2	2	2	3
	3	1	6	2
	4	4	5	1

Hint: introduce a 'dummy destination' with a requirement equal to spare capacity.

(a)   Find a 'least-cost-first' solution and a VAM solution.
(b)   Find an optimal solution. Is it unique?
(c)   By how much would total transportation costs be reduced if one more unit could be made available at origin 4 and one less at origin 2?
(d)   At which of the three destinations would it be cheapest to meet increased requirements, and how much would it cost?

2   Before the advent of natural gas, the West Midlands Gas Board used to purchase coal from about 57 pits in order to supply 22 gasworks. An important problem was to decide to which plant the coal from each pit should be shipped in order to minimise the total transportation costs. OR techniques were developed which eventually saved about £25,000 per year, or approximately 1% of total transport costs. The following is a small-scale prototype problem. (Details of this example are taken from P. Bishop, *The Coal Transportation Problem*, Technical Report OR 5, West Midlands Gas Board, July 1965.)

Suppose the Gas Board has four works which require a total of 4,000 tons of coal per week, as set out in table 1. It has contracted to buy supplies in that amount from four pits as set out also in table 1.

In most cases, coal can be transported from any pit to any works by either road or rail and the transportation costs by each of these two methods is set out in table 2. However, works 3 can receive coal only by road and works 4 can receive coal only by rail. In addition, pit 4 can ship only by rail. Assume that, apart from these restrictions, the cheapest method of transport may be used.

There is a second difficulty in that coal from certain pits is unsuitable for use in certain works, as indicated by the letter 'U' in table 2.

Table 1   Present availabilities and requirements*

Pit	Contracted purchases	Gasworks	Requirements
1	8	1	6
2	14	2	15
3	15	3	12
4	3	4	7
Total	40	Total	40

*in 100 tons per week.

Table 2   Pit to works transportation costs*

From pit	To works by road: 1	2	3	4	by rail 1	2	3	4
1	121	U	100	—	96	U	—	98
2	U	99	U	—	U	81	—	85
3	U	100	100	—	U	78	—	81
4	—	—	—	—	80	80	—	84

* in £ per 100 tons (including, where appropriate, extra handling costs.)

(a)   Under the present contract, what is the cheapest pattern of transporting the coal from the pits to the works while meeting the above restrictions?

(b)   The Gas Board suspects that rather more coal could be made available at certain pits if it were to bargain with the Coal Board. At which pits should it press for the available limits to be raised? If necessary, what increased price per ton on supplies above this limit should it be prepared to concede?

(c)   At the same time, the Gas Board realises there might be possibilities of rearranging production between its own works. What savings in coal transportation costs would be achieved by rearranging the first few units of production?

3   Ajax Ltd is a manufacturer of confectionary. Its production is seasonal with a peak just before Christmas. The company purchases packing cartons from a supplier at a price of £100 per thousand, paying cash on delivery. (Deliveries are made on the first day of each month.) There are no storage costs, but the cost of capital to Ajax is currently 24% per annum. This means that Ajax saves approximately £2 per thousand cartons for every month by which purchases can be delayed, which is equivalent to a £2 per thousand per month discount after September. For this reason Ajax has traditionally purchased cartons in the amount required each month. However, the supplier also has seasonal production problems, and offers discounts on cartons supplied in the supplier's own off-seasons. Column 1 of the accompanying table sets out Ajax Ltd's schedule of monthly requirements of cartons for the next six months. Column 2 sets out the supplier's percentage discount policy. Ajax will have an initial stock of 15,000 cartons at the beginning of September, and wishes to have at least 10,000 cartons in stock at the end of February. The maximum quantity which the supplier can make available in any month is 25,000 cartons.

Month	Ajax Ltd's production requirements	Supplier's price discount
September	13,000	6%
October	22,000	3%
November	25,000	—
December	15,000	—
January	8,000	5%
February	6,000	6%

(a)   Formulate this problem as a transportation problem and set out the tableau.
(b)   Determine the six-month purchasing schedule for Ajax Ltd which minimises present value of cash outflows. Evaluate the benefits to Ajax of: (i) changing its own production schedule; (ii) pursuading the supplier to increase his maximum supply.

7
Network Applications in US Industry and Government

D D KLINGMAN AND F GLOVER

1 Production planning in a US automobile company

The plant executives of a major US automobile company meet every three months (and often more frequently) to establish plant production levels for the next quarter. Since these executives must deal with a multitude of details, their deliberations in the past often proved to be extremely time-consuming and did not always lead to ideal results. Plans were met with counter-plans in a tedious spiral of feedback and incremental change that only gradually converged. Typically, pressures of time forced the process to end before a truly satisfactory operating policy was decided upon. Moreover, because each proposed alternative customarily required several days of calculations to measure its effect on company profit, the number of alternatives explored was often extremely limited.

It was decided to develop a computer-based model to aid in these production-planning and distribution decisions. A requirement of the model was that it should provide within a very short time answers to questions of the form 'what if we do this?'. In this way the executives would be able to speed up discussion of their assumptions, goals and plans.

A model of trans-shipment type was found to be most appropriate. Figure 1 provides a small-scale illustration of the situation. The problem is to determine the number of auto-

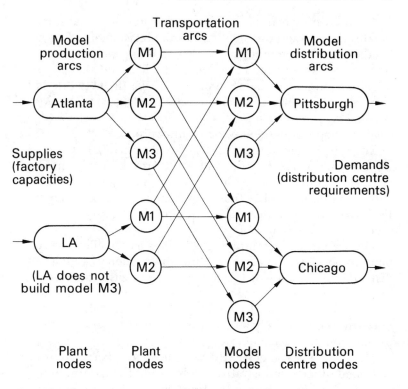

Figure 1. Production planning and distribution model for an automobile manufacturer

mobiles of each of the three models (M1, M2, and M3) to produce at the Atlanta and Los Angeles plants and then to determine how many of each of these models to ship from each plant to the distribution centres in Pittsburgh and Chicago. The objective is to identify a production–distribution plan that minimises total cost.

Supplies at the Atlanta and LA nodes indicate the total production capacities at those plants. Demands at the Pittsburgh and Chicago nodes indicate the total requirements at those distribution centres. Upper and lower bounds may be placed on the arcs to indicate capacity restrictions or minimum requirements for particular types of models at particular plants or distribution centres.

An interesting feature of this model is not only that it coordinates the production and distribution decision, but that it handles a multi-commodity problem in a single-commodity framework. That is, the three nodes M1, M2, and M3 refer to distinct commodities being shipped through the network, but their identities never get mixed or confused, as could be possible in some network models. This illustrates the importance of getting an appropriate network formulation.

The typical size of this problem for a particular division of the company is 1,200 nodes and 4,000 arcs. By using an efficient trans-shipment code[1] the solution time was reduced from about 15 minutes to less than 20 seconds on the company's IBM 370/145 computer. (The requirement of computer memory was also halved.)

This efficiency in computing solutions has enabled the company to develop an on-line real-time production planning and distribution system which is linked to an English language input processor and a graphic display terminal. Answers to the 'what if?' questions are quickly obtained and evaluated. In fact, the executives are typically able to evaluate up to two hundred production plans each quarter.

The system is also currently being used for planning purposes at several other administrative levels within the corporation. Once the executive branch has fixed the production levels of each plant, the production managers and distribution managers then use the network system to determine weekly production schedules for each plant and to arrange with transport firms for shipment of the cars to their final destinations. This phase of the planning process usually requires that the network model be solved several times because:

1   The initial demands for the cars used in the model are only estimates. As the real demands become known, the model must be revised.

2   It may not be possible to contract for shipment of the cars in the manner specified by the solution to the model. Bounds may have to be changed on certain transportation arcs and the model re-run.

3   For various reasons, the plant may not be able to meet the production levels specified by the solution to the model.

Bounds on the production arcs may have to be changed and the model re-run.

In view of these and other considerations previously mentioned, the company has found the on-line interactive network system to be an excellent decision aid for coping with its production scheduling and distribution difficulties.

2   The nature of network problems

It has already been pointed out that transportation and network models are particular types of mathematical programming problems; we shall study the latter in the next chapter. Networks have constituted one of the most significant classes of problems since the inception of mathematical programming. In 1956 a survey by L. W. Smith, Jr[3] indicated that at least half of the linear programming applications involved network models. Some of the reasons cited by the pioneers of mathematical programming for the surprising concentrations on problems of this kind, particularly in applications, are:

1   Answers to 'large' network problems can be computed by hand, which is an impossible task for general linear programming problems of similar dimensions.

2   Many linear programmes can be approximated by simpler network problems.

3   A number of seemingly unrelated linear programmes have been found to be equivalent to network problems.

4   Computer codes were developed as early as 1952 for solving such problems.

5   Many business executives find network models intuitively more understandable; this leads to increased demand for their applications in practical settings.

Over the last twenty years several hundred articles have been written on modelling and solving problems as networks. As suggested in the last chapter, network models have been extensively used in such areas as production and distribution scheduling, financial planning, project selection, facilities location and resource management. In fact, in the 1970's these 'simple' models have gained rather than lost ground to more sophisticated models.

New computer codes have succeeded in solving network problems with an efficiency many times beyond that of codes previously available. Problems that were 'too large' or 'too difficult' to accommodate even as recently as 1970 can now be handled on a routine basis. For example, a network problem with 1,000 nodes and 7,000 arcs can now be solved in eight seconds on an IBM 360/65 using the highly efficient network code of Glover et al.[1] The cost for such a computer run is about one dollar. To solve such a problem using the best commercial linear programming code would take about 20 minutes and cost $200. Another important advantage of network codes is that they typically require very little computer memory. For instance, to solve a 1,000 node, 7,000 arc problem would require less than 90K bytes of memory on an IBM 360/65. Moreover, as the previous section has shown, the combined advances in solution speed and reduced computer memory requirements have recently made it practical to solve network problems by interactive on-line computers linked to graphic display terminal devices.

Many organisations are still unaware of these advances. Significant opportunities to reduce costs and increase returns have thereby been passed by. Yet it is not difficult to identify key operating problems that can be profitably treated in the network framework. In fact, the use of such a framework often makes it easier to visualise important interrelationships that might otherwise go unrecognised, thus leading to the discovery of additional opportunities for improved operations. The purpose of the remainder of this chapter is to acquaint the reader with some real-world problems which our ARC consulting group has identified, modelled and solved as network, assignment, transportation or trans-shipment problems.

3   Some recent applications*

1   A network model is currently being used by a large US corporation to handle its cash-flow transactions. This model

*The references in this section to linear, nonlinear, quadratic, integer and chance-constrained programming will be explained in the next chapter.

indentifies the most economical way to manage receivables and payables. (Similar models have been developed for the banking industry, aiding in the planning of loans, purchases and sales of securities, etc.) This was originally a transportation problem with additional linear constraints but an appropriate transformation yielded a larger transportation problem without the additional constraints. The size of the problem is immense, involving 1,000 origins, 1,000 destinations, and 500,000 cells (arcs). This problem can now be solved in 15 minutes on an IBM 360/65 at a cost of about $150. Allowing an optimistic estimate, a good commercial linear programming code would require somewhat more than 40 hours of central processing time to solve this problem, incurring a cost of $24,000.

2   A trans-shipment model is being used by the Texas Water Development Board for scheduling dam reservoir levels in order to satisfy the peak seasonal demands of each region. This model is solved several thousand times each month in order to simulate all future contingencies over a 36-month planning horizon.

3   A manufacturing model used by a clothes manufacturer involves a two-stage trans-shipment model. The first stage involves the acquisition of cloth inventories from textile manu-facturers. Once this inventory is ascertained, it becomes the supply of the second phase which determines which trousers are to be produced and which sew lines (production lines) are to cut them. The final formulation is a transportation problem with 150 origins, 1,200 destinations, and 20,000 cells. The typical solution time is three minutes on a UNIVAC 1106 at a cost of $25.

4   A model used by New Mexico Department of Agriculture determines, over a sequence of time periods, the planting, picking and storing of cotton at various farms, and the distribu-tion of cotton to various gins. The problem is complicated by significant fixed charges, seasonal power costs and higher over-time labour costs at the cotton gins. The 'natural' formulation of this problem yields a mixed-integer transportation problem with additional linear constraints. The transportation part of this formulation involves 2,000 origins, 2,300 destinations and

2,460,000 cells, but the overall complexity of the model prevented its solution in this form. However, this problem was equivalently formulated as a plant location and trans-shipment model consisting of 3,441 nodes, 61,640 arcs and 20 0—1 variables. A hybrid code[2] made it possible to solve this problem in less than a half-hour of central processing time on a CDC-6600 at a cost of $300.

5   The US Department of the Treasury has two statistical data base files, *Current Population Survey* and *Statistics of Income*. Each record on these files contains descriptions of a family type and an indication of the number of families in the US population of this type. The files are extensively used to analyse the effect on federal revenue of various policy changes, such as welfare payment levels, social security benefits, income tax rates, etc. To analyse fully the effect of these changes, it is necessary to use some of the information in both of the files. It is desirable to have a method which limits the amount of information lost as the original files are merged for a particular policy evaluation.

This problem can be formulated as a transportation problem, by thinking of each record in each file as a node. The 'supply' or 'demand' associated with a given node corresponds to the number of families represented by the associated record. An arc connecting two nodes indicates that it is reasonable to consider merging the two associated records. The 'cost' coefficient on each arc is a measure of the common information characteristics of the two records. The flow along any arc is interpreted as the number of families to be represented by that merged record. Thus, solving the transportation problem yields the specifications for a merged file which minimises the information lost in the process. These specifications include (a) the number of records to be contained in the merged file, (b) which records are to be merged with each other and (c) the number of families represented by each merged record.

An extended transportation system has been designed for the Treasury which is capable of solving a problem of the above type with 50,000 nodes and 62.5 million arcs. A full-size problem has not yet been generated so the solution time is unknown, but a prototype problem with 5,000 nodes and

625,000 arcs was solved on a UNIVAC-1108 in less than nine minutes of total job time (including all input and output processing). In problems of this magnitude, the intimate coordination of modelling and computer solution effort is indispensible.

4 Conclusion

In this chapter, we have illustrated how networks can be used to model many diverse decision-making situations. Like all modelling efforts, the creation of an appropriate network model for a particular problem requires a blend of experience, skill and imagination. Fortunately, the inherent pictorial characteristic of network models contributes enormously to the ease with which important relationships can be captured, visualised and communicated to others. As emphasised in Chapter 2, it is unnecessary to be able to specify all problem characteristics in a rigorous mathematical sense at the outset of constructing a network model; one may simply sketch the problem pictorially and use parenthetical annotations to maintain important characteristics in view while the crucial interrelationships are singled out. Next, one tries to identify the best formulation and the appropriate method of solution. At this stage, the intimate coordination of modelling techniques and computer solution methods can be especially beneficial.

One further characteristic of network models not possessed by other models should be pointed out. Because of the solution speed of network codes, it is often not crucial for the model to include *all* the interrelationships of the real decision problem. Many of the interrelationships can be adequately (and sometimes better) handled by solving the model several times using different parameter values. This provides a *dynamic* sensitivity analysis in which the decision maker is able to participate fully. He can test the implications of alternative assumptions and strategies and thereby mould an effective policy for achieving his objectives.

References and further reading

1   Glover F., Karney D. and Klingman D. 'Implementation and computational comparisons of primal, dual and primal—dual computer

codes for minimum cost network flow problems', *Networks*, vol. 4, no. 3, 1974.

2   Glover F., Karney D. and Klingman D., *Development and Computational Testing on Large Scale Primal Simplex Network Codes*, CS Report 281, Center for Cybernetic Studies, University of Texas, Austin, Texas, 78712, 1975.

3   Smith L. W., Jr, 'Current status of the industrial use of linear programming', *Management Science*, vol. 2, 1956.

8
Linear Programming

S C LITTLECHILD

1 Introduction

Linear programming (LP) is a mathematical technique which is particularly useful in a situation where there are decisions to be made about many variables (for example, the levels of production at each factory of a whole product line) and where there are numerous constraints relating to the availability of resources (for example, machine capacity, storage space, labour availability, etc.). The difficulty is that the decisions interact: if the production of item A is expanded this week, then the limited capacity might require production of item B to be cut back, but this in turn might free some skilled labour to work on product C, and so on. Linear programming is an attempt to aid the decision-maker in evaluating these multiple interdependencies.

Some of the practical situations in which linear programming has been found useful are:

1 Production planning (performed quarterly for the next 12 months) in Hoogovens Steel Company, encompassing production levels at each plant, size of stocks on hand, transportation requirements, raw material inputs and supporting activities. Similar applications have been made in many large firms. One such application at Heinz Ltd is described in detail in the next chapter.

2   Agricultural planning by ICI Farm Advisory Service for large arable and livestock farms to decide most profitable production patterns in the light of acreage available, crop rotation and animal food requirements, labour and machinery constraints, building capacities, capital limitations, etc.

3   The formulation of animal feed products at J. Bibby & Sons Ltd to ensure that the cheapest combination of raw materials is being used which meets the required nutritional specifications. This is a classic problem which stimulated one of the very first research papers on linear programming.

4   The blending of crude oils or molten metals to satisfy certain technical requirements and capacity constraints while maximising profits. It has been suggested, in fact, that almost all the electronic computers used in the oil industry were originally justified on the basis of such blending exercises and were only subsequently applied to other problems.

5   Manpower planning in the US Navy and many large corporations, in order to decide how many new personnel should be hired, at what levels and in what applications, bearing in mind retirement policy, natural wastage, antici-pated growth of business, promotion policy, etc.

6   National planning in many countries to decide levels of production and investment in each industry. Similar applica-tions have been made in particular sectors, particularly education and energy.

We shall illustrate the linear programming approach by means of a very simple example, involving only two variables and three constraints. This will enable us to represent and solve the model graphically before representing and solving it algebraically. (Modern computers using efficient solution codes are able to solve problems involving thousands of variables and constraints in a matter of minutes.) We shall then explore some aspects of sensitivity analysis, and introduce the 'dual' problem. Finally, we refer to some of the extensions known as non-linear, integer, and stochastic programming which considerably increase the flexibility of this technique.

2   An example

A farmer has available 100 acres of land which he can plant with either wheat or potatoes, or leave it fallow. Taking into account expected yields, crop prices, planting and harvesting costs (including labour) etc., he calculates that his net profit will be £90 per acre for wheat and £60 per acre for potatoes. On average it takes 6 man-hours per acre to harvest wheat and 3 man-hours per acre to harvest potatoes. During the critical autumn harvesting period he will have only 480 man-hours of help available. His maximum acreage quota for potatoes is 65 acres. Assuming the farmer wants to maximise profits, what acreage should he plant of each crop?

This problem is sufficiently simple that we can represent it graphically as in figure 1. Let the horizontal axis represent the acreage of wheat planted and let the vertical axis refer to potatoes. Any point on the graph then represents a particular planting pattern. Let us first delimit which areas on the graph correspond to **feasible** planting patterns, i.e. ones which do not violate any of the known restrictions. First, since it does not make sense to plant negative acreages, the chosen pattern must be above the horizontal axis and to the right of the vertical axis. The maximum acreage constraint on potatoes is a horizontal straight line; the chosen production point must not lie above this line, as the arrow indicates. A simple constraint of this kind is known as an **upper bound**. A straight line drawn between the 100-acre points on each axis represents all patterns of planting which take up exactly 100 acres, so the chosen point must be on or below this line. Finally, if no potatoes were planted, it would be possible to harvest up to 480/6 = 80 acres of wheat, and if no wheat were planted, it would be possible to harvest up to 480/3 = 160 acres of potatoes. A straight line joining these two points comprises all the planting patterns which require exactly 480 hours of labour, so the chosen point must lie on or below this line.

The **feasible region** is the set of points which satisfy *all* constraints, and is shaded on the graph. Which of these points is the most profitable? Let us begin by plotting the set of planting patterns corresponding to some arbitrary level of total profit — say £3,000. This could be achieved with $33\frac{1}{3}$ acres of wheat and no

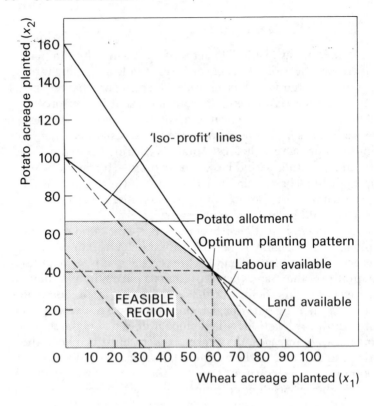

Figure 1. Graphical representation of farmer's crop-planting problem

potatoes, or by 50 acres of potatoes and no wheat, or in fact by any (linear) combination of these two points — for example $16\frac{2}{3}$ acres of wheat and 25 acres of potatoes. Draw in the straight line corresponding to £3,000 profit. This is sometimes called an 'iso-profit' (equal-profit) line. Note that some of the points in the feasible region lie on it, and so yield a profit of £3,000. Now repeat the procedure for £6,000. The second line is evidently parallel to the first and lies above and to the right of it. It, too, contains some points from the feasible region. This suggests that if we take a ruler, hold it parallel to the iso-profit curves and move it as far to the right as possible without going completely outside the feasible region, then we shall have found that feasible production pattern which yields the greatest total profit. In fact, this optimal point is to be found at a 'corner' of the feasible region where the acreages may be read off the graph as 60 acres wheat and 40 acres potatoes, yielding a total profit of £7,800.

Note that all the lines which we have drawn are straight. This explains the term 'linear' programming.

3   Algebraic formulation

It would not be difficult to represent additional constraints on this graph, but if an additional crop were considered then the graph would need three dimensions (and the constraint lines would become constraint planes). With four or more variables, graphical representation is impossible, and a mathematical approach is required. (Alternatively, by plotting resources along the axes, it is possible to represent graphically as rays from the origin any number of variables, but only two constraints can then be incorporated.) In fact, it is not difficult at all to represent the problem algebraically.

Let x_1 and x_2 be variables denoting the number of acres planted of wheat and potatoes, respectively. Bearing in mind the expected profits per acre for each crop, the total profit will be

$$90x_1 + 60x_2$$

This expression is known as the **objective function**. We wish to choose x_1 and x_2 to maximise the objective function subject to the following constraints:

land available $x_1 + x_2 \leqslant 100$
harvest labour available $6x_1 + 3x_2 \leqslant 480$
potato quota $x_2 \leqslant 65$
non-negative acreages $x_1 \geqslant 0, x_2 \geqslant 0$.

These various mathematical expressions constitute a simple linear programme.

In the present example, we know from the graphical solution that both land and labour are fully utilised, hence we may solve the two equations

$$x_1 + x_2 = 100$$

$$6x_1 + 3x_2 = 480$$

to give $x_1 = 60$, $x_2 = 40$, thereby confirming the solution read off the graph.

Unfortunately, in general we do not know in advance which resources will be fully utilised at the optimum solution. A more systematic mathematical approach is therefore required, as outlined in section 6.

With obvious modifications it is possible to formulate linear programmes which minimise cost instead of maximise profit, or indeed maximise any other objective, and to introduce 'greater than or equal to' or 'equality' constraints as well as 'less than or equal to' ones.

4   Sensitivity analysis

We might be interested not only in solving the problem but also in knowing how the solution would vary if the conditions of the problem were different. For example, perhaps more resources could be made available at a certain price, in which case it would be useful to know by how much profit could be increased by employing these additional resources. Alternatively, different activities might be considered.

Notice that the farmer's most profitable plan involves planting fewer potatoes than his maximum limit. This constraint is said to be **slack**. A small change in the level of this constraint would not affect the optimal solution. On the diagram, if the line corresponding to the slack constraint were shifted slightly, the optimum would not move. The farmer would attach no value (at present) to an increase in the potato quota.

By contrast, all the available land is planted and the harvest-period labour force is expected to be fully employed. These two constraints are said to be **tight** or **binding**. If more or less land or labour were made available, this would affect the optimum planting pattern. However, it would not necessarily alter it in an easily predictable pattern, and consequently the effect on profit may be difficult to calculate.

For example, how much could profit be increased if the farmer had 101 instead of 100 acres? One's first reaction might be that extra land would not be any use without a simultaneous increase in labour. But a glance at figure 1 suggests that if the land constraint were moved outwards slightly, the optimum point would move slightly up the labour constraint line. In other words, the acreage of potatoes would increase but the acreage of wheat would *decrease*. To measure the exact effect, solve the equations

$$x_1 + x_2 = 101$$

$$6x_1 + 3x_2 = 480$$

to yield $x_1 = 59$, $x_2 = 62$. The reduction of one acre of wheat frees not only one acre of land but also six hours of labour. Taken together with the new acre of land this allows two extra acres of potatoes to be planted and harvested. The effect on total profits is (2 acres @ £60) − (1 @ £90) = £30. In other words, an extra acre of land brings in an extra profit of £30 if the planting pattern is suitably reorganised. This value of £30 is often referred to as the **shadow price** or **opportunity cost** of land. (Recall the discussion of shadow prices in Chapter 6.)

Two further points should be made. First, this value applies equally to a decrease in acreage available. There would be a drop in profits of £30 per acre withdrawn. Second, this value applies only to small changes in acreage. Thus, as acreage is increased one could substitute two acres of potatoes for one acre of wheat only until the acreage allotment of 65 acres of potatoes was reached, viz. after five acres have been added. Subsequent acres cannot be utilized, so they bring no extra profit to the farm. Similarly, as acres are withdrawn the farmer will switch to wheat, but only until potato acreage drops to zero after 20 acres have been withdrawn. After that, the wheat acreage itself has to be reduced at a loss in profit of £90 per acre. In general, the value of an extra unit of any resource decreases as the availability of that resource increases (so that the value of an extra unit increases as the total availability decreases). These changes in shadow prices occur in discrete steps as the corresponding resources are varied. (It is instructive to plot the shadow price of land against the amount of land available.)

5   Sensitivity analysis: new activities

We could go through a similar exercise to work out the value of extra labour, but a more general approach is preferable. Let u_1, u_2 and u_3 denote the value to the farmer of, respectively, an additional acre of land, an additional hour of labour and an additional acre of potato quota. These values are precisely the shadow prices just referred to. We wish to calculate u_1, u_2 and u_3. We already know that u_3 is zero, because the present potato quota is not fully utilised. Now one acre of land plus six hours of labour must be worth *at least* £90, because those are the inputs necessary to generate a profit of £90 by planting an acre of wheat. But we know that these resources cannot be worth *more* than £90 otherwise it would not be worth planting wheat, and we already know it is worth doing that. Hence we have

$$1u_1 + 6u_2 = £90$$

By an exactly similar argument with reference to potatoes we deduce that

$$1u_1 + 3u_2 = £60$$

These two simultaneous equations are easily solved to yield u_1 = £30 and u_2 = £10. The first value coincides, as expected, with our previous calculations of the value of land. The second value says that extra labour at harvest time is worth £10 per hour. This suggests that it would pay the farmer to hire extra labour for the harvest period, providing he could get it for less than £10 per hour above normal rates. This would enable him to substitute some wheat, which is a more profitable but also a more labour-intensive crop, for some potatoes.

Suppose an acre of peas requires only two hours of labour at harvest time but generates a profit of only £40 per acre. Would it be worth planting peas? Here the shadow prices come in handy again. In order to plant and harvest peas the acreage of wheat and/or potatoes will have to be reduced, at a consequent reduction in profit. Will this outweigh the profit on peas? An acre of peas requires one acre of land and two hours of labour. We have already calculated that the value of land in growing present crops is £30 per acre and the value of labour is £10 per hour. The resources necessary to grow peas therefore have a value of

$$(1 @ £30) + (2 @ £10) = £50$$

in growing present crops. This would not be compensated for by the profit on peas. However, if the profit on peas were to increase to over £50 per acre, then it would be profitable to introduce peas and to reduce one of the other crops. Unfortunately, we cannot tell without further calculation exactly what the new pattern of activities would be.

6   Running a linear programme

Solving even small linear programmes is a tedious procedure best left to a computer. A most important solution algorithm, called the Simplex method, for many years formed the basis of most computer codes. The principle of this algorithm may be simply stated. As figure 1 suggests, if all the constraints and the objective function are linear, then, whatever the numbers involved, the optimal solution will always lie at a 'corner' or **extreme point** of the feasible region. (If the objective function is parallel to a constraint, then all points along this constraint within the feasible region are optimal, including both corners.) The Simplex method starts at one extreme point of the feasible region and moves to an adjacent corner, then to another adjacent corner, and so on, always one step at a time, and always in a direction which improves profit, until the optimum is attained. Each move is called an **iteration**. The similarity between this Simplex method and the row-column sum method is not surprising. We shall see in section 7 exactly how transportation problems are a special case of linear programming problems.

Nowadays linear programmes often involve many hundreds or even thousands of constraints. Because the power of computers is increasing and more efficient codes are being developed, the problem of computing the optimal solution to a linear programme is no longer the critical difficulty. It is, rather, the collection, inputting and revision of data and the interpretation of results. In the first instance, time is not well spent making sure that every coefficient is absolutely correct. Many resources or constraints will not be binding, and many variables or activities will not be utilised. Attention should be focused on those parts of the system which are critical. Sensitivity analysis will show what margin or error can be tolerated in the computation of each profit or resource availability. As regards data input and output, the usual procedure nowadays is to write (or hire) a separate computer programme, called a **matrix generator,** which takes the data in a form convenient to the user and transforms it into a form convenient for the computer. Another programme, called a **report writer** transforms the linear programming results into a format specified by the manager — for example, involving tables or graphs.

7   Transportation problems as linear programmes

The farm problem discussed earlier in the chapter can be set out in the following way. Single rows or columns of figures are called **vectors**; the rectangular block of coefficients is called a **matrix**.

x_1	x_2		
90	60	=	max
1	1	⩽	100
6	3	⩽	480
0	1	⩽	65

A transportation problem may be represented as a linear programme if we define the variable x_{ij} as the number of units shipped from origin i to destination j. The constraint on availability of capacity at origin 1 of the example in Chapter 6 would be written

$$x_{11} + x_{12} + x_{13} + x_{14} = 20$$

and the constraint on requirements at the first destination would be

$$x_{11} + x_{21} + x_{31} = 11$$

The whole problem can be represented in matrix form as follows: The blanks indicate zeros, which have been omitted for clarity.

x_{11}	x_{12}	x_{13}	x_{14}	x_{21}	x_{22}	x_{23}	x_{24}	x_{31}	x_{32}	x_{33}	x_{34}		
1	6	3	6	7	3	1	6	9	4	5	4	=	min
1	1	1	1									=	20
				1	1	1	1					=	10
								1	1	1	1	=	25
1				1				1				=	11
	1				1				1			=	13
		1				1				1		=	17
			1				1				1	=	14

Notice that the matrix of coefficients is very **dense** (i.e. has few zeros) for the first linear programme (the farm problem) but is very **sparse** for the transportation problem. Moreover, the non-zero coefficients in the transportation matrix are all 1's arranged in a striking pattern. It is this special structure which makes transportation problems about a hundred times more easy to solve than arbitrary linear programmes of the same size, as emphasised in the previous chapter. Typically, in a large linear programme not more than 5% of the coefficients are non-zero. The next chapter discusses how advantage was taken of this type of special structure in the production problem at Heinz.

8 Extensions of linear programming

Linear programming is in fact a very flexible technique. There are a number of extensions and modifications, which collectively go by the name of mathematical programming, which may be used to model a great variety of situations. We shall briefly discuss a few of these.

(a) Non-linear programming   For a single farmer, the price which he gets per ton of crop is essentially independent of the volume of his sales, because of this his production is small compared with the total market and therefore does not influence price. For other firms this might not be so — in order to sell more they would need to reduce price and per unit profit. The objective function becomes a non-linear expression instead of a linear one. Graphically, this would be represented by a family of iso-profit curves which were not straight lines. In the same way, situations of increasing or decreasing returns to scale give rise to non-linear constraints. It is possible to solve such models, but by no means as efficiently as one can solve linear programmes. Accordingly, one often looks for linear approximation — for example, by dividing a sales variable into several new variables, each with upper bounds, corresponding to different sales volumes and having different prices.

(b) Integer programming   Linear programmes involve decisions about **continuous** variables, such as the level of production. In practice, one often has to make decisions about **discrete** variables, such as the number of aircraft to purchase, where the solution must be limited to **integer** values (whole numbers). In particular, many decisions are of the 'yes' or 'no' (or **logical**) variety, such as whether or not build a factory in a particular location. The variables take only the values zero (no) or one (yes). Algorithms are available for solving such problems, but their efficiency seems to depend heavily upon the structure of the problem. National Westminster Bank used integer programming to decide which (if any) of a number of staff training centres should be kept open. The technique is regularly used for aircrew and machine scheduling, for minimising waste in cutting up paper and timber, and for locating depots in distribution networks as described in the previous two chapters.

(c) Programming under uncertainty   It may be that not all the elements in a linear programme are sufficiently well-known to

be represented by a single number, particularly if the problem involves long-term planning. For example, it might be desired to provide sufficient capacity to meet demand next year, but the level of the latter is quite uncertain. The importance of this problem in oil companies led to the development of **chance-constraints**, which are required to hold only with a specified probability (say 97%). After estimating the relevant probability distribution, the chance-constraint may generally be reduced to a normal linear constraint known as a **deterministic equivalent**. In the illustration just given, the oil company is effectively constrained to provide capacity to meet demand in a 3/100 winter (i.e. a winter so severe that it occurs on average only three times in every hundred years). More sophisticated versions involve **decision rules** for choosing future actions according to the outcome of events as yet unknown. Chance-constrained programming models have been used by American marketing firms to decide whether or not to go ahead with new products, where and how far to test-market, how to design the marketing strategy, etc. Other models, known by the names of **linear programming under uncertainty, programming with recourse, stochastic programming**, etc. have been used to determine efficient financial portfolios with specified risk levels and to design water resource systems of reservoirs and canals.

References and further reading

1   Charnes A. and Cooper W. W., *Management Models and Industrial Applications of Linear Programming* (2 vols), Wiley 1961.

2   Sasieni M., Yaspan A. and Friedman L., *Operations Research: Methods and Problems*, Wiley 1959.

3   Wagner H. M., *Principles of Operations Research*, Prentice Hall 1969.

Exercises

1   Recalculate the optimal solution to the farm example in the text on the assumption that the potato allotment is only 35 acres. What are the new shadow prices?

2   A smallholder owns six acres of land and wishes to decide
what proportion to plant with flowers and what proportion
with strawberries. He calculates the average return (that is,
proceeds of sale less costs of bulbs/plants and fertilisers, etc.)
to be £80 per acre for flowers and £100 per acre for strawberries.
However, the time he has available for cultivation and picking is
somewhat limited, and the labour requirements by season are as
follows (in man-hours per acre):

| | Season: | | | |
Crop	Winter	Spring	Summer	Autumn
Flowers	10	40	0	10
Strawberries	10	20	50	10
Labour available (hours)	100	200	200	100

(a)   What pattern of crops would you recommend the smallholder to grow?
(b)   How much would you recommend he be willing to pay
for extra labour during each season?
(c)   Formulate and interpret the dual to this problem.

3 (Due to A. W. McCurdy)   Rover Division of British Leyland
Company regularly uses a linear programme for scheduling car
production. The following is a brief outline of the model.
Attempt to formulate algebraically a small-scale version.
    The objective of the LP is to select orders for production
taking into account sales priorities and production control
constraints. Orders are assigned priorities based on the type of
order and the length of time they have been in the outstanding
order bank. Production constraints such as overall mix of models
to preserve line balancing are fed in, together with production
control constraints on availability of major units, e.g. engines.
Periodically the mainframe computer is used to select several
shifts of orders so as to maximise the total 'priority score' while
complying with the constraints. These orders are passed across

to a mini-computer which is used to schedule orders on an hourly basis on the assembly line. The LP matrix is quite large, containing thousands of columns, reflecting the large number of model variants. There are 200–300 rows. The run time is of the order of 15–20 minutes.

9

Production Planning at Heinz

D R KAYE AND A M DUNSMUIR

1   Introduction

This chapter describes the development and implementation of a production and distribution planning system, utilising linear programming techniques, which was installed at H. J. Heinz Co. Ltd. The system took between three and four years to develop and install, during which time it cost the Company in excess of £100,000. Since late 1970 it has been used every quarter to produce most of the Company's production plan for the period up to 18 months ahead. It has been estimated that since implementation the system has been saving the Company more than £300,000 (in operating costs and in the release of capital) per annum.

The planning system is supported by an extensive data processing system containing all the necessary information on costs, recipes, capacities and so on, which is maintained on the Company's ICL System 4/50. From the basic information provided by this system, a 3,000 equation by 8,000 variable linear programme (representing the production and distribution requirements and alternatives over the next 12 to 18 months) is generated and then partially solved at an IBM service bureau. The output from the linear programme is then transferred back to the in-house System 4/50, where it is used by a suite of scheduling programmes to generate a shift-by-shift production plan over the period being considered. From this plan are produced reports of weekly requirements of materials, of the numbers needed in each of the various labour groups, of the utilisation of each major piece of equipment in the factories, and of the inventory levels, by product, implied by the sales forecasts and the production plan. These reports are passed to the relevant management in head office and the Company's three factories as a basis for developing coordinated and detailed operating schedules. Throughout the quarter, as circumstances change, the plan is regularly updated to ensure that the Company continues to operate its production facilities as closely as possible to minimum costs.

The system is big, complex, depends on esoteric techniques, and took a long time to build; nevertheless the implementation was successful and the resulting system effective. In this chapter we shall try to identify why. But before reflecting on the strategy of the project's development, we shall summarise some key features of the planning problem and then indicate the main steps of its solution.

2   Background

Allowing for the different sizes in which many varieties are made, H. J. Heinz Co. Ltd manufactures several hundred distinct stock items and fills several million cans and bottles every day. This is done in two large factories in the North of England and one in the South. Although some products can be made in only one factory, most of the high volume products are made in both the North and the South. There are some 50 filling lines dispersed over the three factories, each filling line handling a broadly similar group of foods. Most products can be filled on any of several lines, a few on as many as 10. Some operations cannot be performed simultaneously with others, either for technological reasons or because of capacity constraints on shared facilities. Thus there are a large number of manufacturing choices constrained in more or less complex ways, and each costing a different amount.

The filling lines are planned to be run for prescribed periods, which are based on the shift patterns. Between these periods, equipment must be washed down and changes of can size effected where appropriate. Thus set-up times are not a problem, but the production schedule must recognise the need to produce in multiples of 'period-loads'.

There is seasonality in demand, more pronounced in some varieties than in others; there are considerable peaks in sales caused by the Company's marketing activities; the price, quality and availability of raw materials have a high degree of seasonality. Most of the finished goods can be stored for a fairly long time but, quite apart from the financial penalty of tying-up working capital in unnecessarily high stock levels, there is a company policy of not exceeding a maximum storage time before distribution. Thus there is considerable choice as to what times in the year each product should be manufactured in a batch which could be as short as a shift or as long as a month or more, and the costs of these choices are different.

The labour requirement is different for different product mixes; there is a high degree of flexibility in how labour is used. However, as one might expect, the degree by which overall labour availability can be expected to change from one period to the next is severely restricted. It is, therefore, necessary to plan production in such a way that the variation in labour levels from month to month falls within fairly tightly defined limits.

Finally, there is uncertainty as to the eventual realisation of planned production rates, sales levels, raw material prices, yields and availability, labour levels, and machine capacity.

3   Defining the problem

Before the implementation of the planning system, the company had carried out the operation, manually, on a quarterly basis. This manually produced plan was arrived at through a detailed shift-scheduling exercise worked backwards in time from the end of the period. The rationale behind this approach was that, by operating on a shift-by-shift basis, feasibility could be guaranteed while working backwards should ensure that products would be manufactured as late as possible in relation to their future sales, and so the finished-goods inventory level would be kept low. This plan was the basis for forward ordering of supplies, delivery to specified factories, retiming or marketing activity necessitated by production capacity problems, financing of stocks, and planning of labour levels. Every two weeks, the next 10 weeks of the plan would be updated to provide the basis for daily shift planning at the factories. The aim of the central planning operation was to provide successively updated, broadly feasible production plans in line with the marketing department's most up-to-date estimates of sales, and in a way which was consistent with qualitative economic guidelines. However, although the resulting plans would be consistent with the central planners' perceptions of shift scheduling details, these perceptions were frequently at variance with the facts in the factories. Furthermore, in the very complex, multi-choice environment of the problem, the search for the cheapest feasible plan could not be pursued very far with the low level of iterative capability inherent in the manual approach.

The planning problem indicated above was clearly an interesting one for computerisation. The objective of such computerisation was seen as being the identification of a production plan which, for any set of marketing requirements, would be significantly cheaper to operate than the manually produced plan; would also be at least as feasible and at least as responsive to changes in estimates of demand, price, and production capacity; and would be at least no slower to produce than the manual plan.

In assessing this problem, we first contended that the varying economics of the interactions between factories and between time periods were difficult to cope with manually and therefore could well be a major source of potential cost savings in a computerised system. Secondly, we observed that capacity constraints not only varied with the characteristics of the individual products being produced, but, because of the flexibility in the use of labour, depended to a large extent on the entire range of products being manufactured at any time. Together, these two observations led to the contention that the planning model would have simultaneously to consider all factories, all distribution areas, all products and all time periods up to the planning horizon. But this would have given us an impossibly big and unwieldy model to work on, particularly since a large subset of the constraints were logical, and therefore integer, in character. Our approach to the problem thus created

had therefore to be in two stages. First, we would build a large
— but not too large — linear programming model which would
be designed to generate that allocation of production to factories
and filling lines for a number of two- or three-month periods
up to the planning horizon, which would minimise the total of
manufacturing, distribution and inventory holding costs. At
optimal, this model would provide an economically optimal
plan, but this would almost certainly be infeasible because all
short-term constraints (including the need to produce in
multiples of the 'period-loads') had been ignored. The output
of the linear programming model would therefore have to pass
on as input to a set of scheduling programmes which would
split up the production allocations and organise them into shift
schedules which took into account all the short-term constraints
previously ignored. Furthermore, when these constraints were
found to be violated by the linear programming solution, the
scheduling programme would have to operate on the marginal
cost information also available from the linear programme (i.e.
the shadow prices) to find an alternative feasible solution not
much more expensive than the one indicated by the linear
programme. A description of the algorithms used in generating
the final schedules is outside the scope of this chapter, but the
process can, perhaps, best be thought of as a 'cascade' of
optimising models, each one by its solution defining the space
in which its more detailed successor should search for the next
level of solution.

4   Concern for implementation

A number of principles guided our plans for development in
this project:

1   a continued commitment by management, which was
encouraged initially through the establishment of a project
team composed jointly of outside consultants from Arthur
Anderson & Co. and a newly-established internal OR group;
then, once the project was underway, by the phased development of the model so that useful sub-models were made
available to the users from time to time, well before the final
model was ready;

2   the requirement that the output from the model should relate directly to the realities of the production scheduling problem as seen by the users, so that no 'interpretation' of the computer-produced reports would be required;

3   the need for total acceptance of the model's output by the users, without which it would be only too likely to fall into disuse. To this end we planned, from the beginning, that there would be a 'running-in' period — as lengthy as the users cared to demand — when we would work continuously to adapt the logic of the scheduling programme to improve the quality of the schedules being produced, and during which we would not attempt to force the users to accept the system until they had expressed their satisfaction with the plans it was producing. In the event, the users pre-empted us on this point by insisting that the system should be made available to them rather earlier than we considered it to be ready.

5   Construction of the model

Following the above principles, we divided the development of the LP model into three phases:

1   a single-factory, single time-period model, which was useful to us as a check that we understood the production process properly, and was also of some interest to the users in that it provided some insights into the effective use of equipment;

2   a three-factory, single time-period model, again of interest both to the development team and to the users, in that it provided some useful information on the trade-offs available between production and distribution costs;

3   the full multi-factory, multi-time-period model.

The structure of the full model is fairly typical of production and distribution LP models, being a combination of small dense blocks with coefficients which are cumbersome to calculate and much larger, sparse blocks with coefficients of ± 1. Unfortunately, because of the interactions between these two sets of blocks, the simplicity of the latter coefficients is not reflected in any reduction in the computing effort required for solution over a more general model of the same overall size — and at the size of the Heinz model (3,000 by 8,000) many thousands of pounds worth of computing power would have been needed had we not been able to take advantage of an unusual facility available in IBM's MPSX programme.

Briefly, what was done was to have the matrix generation programme guess what the optimal inter-period inventory levels would be at the optimal point. This enabled each period to be solved as a separate problem, greatly reduced in size, and not requiring an excessive amount of machine time. When combined, these solutions provided a feasible solution to the full model. Thus if the inter-period inventory level had been guessed perfectly, the optimal solution to the full problem would have been available immediately, without the requirement for any full-sized iterations. But even if the guesses had been wrong (as they inevitably were), far fewer iterations would be required to find the true optimal solution.

6   Operating experience

In fact, the model never was run to optimal. In practice, a log was kept from iteration to iteration of the value of the objective function and if, over a specified (large) number of iterations, it failed to change by more than a specified percentage, the run was terminated. (It was known that, in any case, the scheduling suite would move away from the continuous optimal point, so there was little need to search for it too accurately.) In this way it was possible to generate quite satisfactory input for the scheduling suite in some four to five hours of IBM 360/65 time — certainly an expensive process, but small compared to the savings over the manually produced plan which were indicated.

After some experience in running the model had been obtained, it was noticed that whereas we had been unable to specify rules which could be used by the matrix generator to calculate inter-period inventory levels consistently close to those generated by the LP, it appeared to be rather simpler to determine, from overall production requirements, how the labour forces would be divided up among the various work-cells in the factories.

The sub-models were therefore re-defined in the form of individual work-cells covering all periods (rather than all work-cells together for single periods) with the linking 'guesses' now being labour allocations rather than inventory levels. This modification resulted in a reduction in the overall amount of machine time needed to get a satisfactory solution by some 50%.

We make this point to impress on the reader the very real requirement for 'hands-on' experience in dealing with large LP models. Slight adjustments to model formulations can have very significant impacts on computing times, and therefore costs. Advice on likely ways of cutting costs will normally be available from LP support staff, if a service bureau or software house is being used. This advice should always be taken. But equally important is the opportunity for experimentation which is offered by a series of runs of an on-going model (in our case quarterly), and which should be accepted whenever this is possible. Such experimentation, although perhaps expensive in the short-term, can show substantial long-term savings, and it is not unknown for a particular model's machine requirements to drop by a factor of three or four as a result of slight adjustments, either to its formulation or to the precise way in which it is run on the computer.

10

Demand Analysis and Short-term Forecasting

C D LEWIS

1   Introduction

In the previous chapters we have discussed methods for scheduling production and planning transportation and distribution systems for a specified pattern of demand. Such demand patterns have to be ascertained or forecast in some way. It will generally not be possible to forecast them with complete accuracy. The next few chapters will therefore discuss techniques such as inventory control, queueing theory, simulation and decision trees which have been developed to handle situations where future demand can at best be expressed in terms of probabilities. The purpose of the present chapter is to describe the chief methods which have been found useful in forecasting demand.

In some situations, production of the manufacturing organisation's final product may be exactly specified in advance, and demand at lower levels of production is totally dependent on demand at the higher level (e.g. one car requires exactly five wheel assemblies). In such situations, demand at the material and component level can be discovered quite simply by **exploding** the known sales programme into the material and component parts, then **aggregating** totals of each part. Techniques such as **materials requirements planning** (MRP), which produces a time schedule of requirements to meet the desired schedule of the finished product, do work successfully and are gaining increasing acceptance. They are particularly useful in, for instance, the specialised machine tool industry where 'build only to order' is the rule. Such techniques fall down very badly, however, should any errors creep into the final product sales programme, simply because the exploding/aggregation approach tends to magnify such errors. This magnification of error depends very much on the number of levels at which inventories are held in the raw material/component/sub-assembly/main assembly/final product chain and it is not unusual to find manufacturers operating with at least twenty such levels.

Where demand at the various levels of production is not interdependent, a valuable approach is to study past values of demand at the appropriate level of production, whether that be raw material, work in progress or finished goods. Such a study may reveal systematic trends within the demand data. If it can be assumed that past demand patterns will be continued into the future, then the extrapolation of those trends can be used to predict future demand. The identification of such trends and the development of predictive models based on them is termed **forecasting.**

Short-term forecasting of demand typically involves forecasting a few days ahead at the level of the retailer, often weeks ahead at the level of the wholesaler and a few months ahead at the level of the manufacturer. For such purposes it is generally sufficient to limit attention to previous demand data, using such methods as **exponential smoothing.**

For purposes of **medium-term** forecasting, relating to the next few months or years, it is generally necessary to relate the demand for the product to various technical, economic and social factors, called **explanatory variables,** and to make independent forecasts of the latter. Examples of this procedure include national income, consumer purchasing powers, levels of prices and employment, population change, etc. **Multiple regression techniques** are found useful here, and a methodology of statistical modelling has been developed which is not unlike the OR methodology described in Chapter 2.

Long-term forecasting, ranging from one year to even a decade ahead, is typically concerned with technological change. The scope for statistical techniques here is more limited, and long-term forecasting itself is still in its infancy.

Although operational researchers are frequently involved in all kinds of forecasting situations, limitations of space preclude a comprehensive treatment here. This chapter will concentrate on short-term forecasting for purposes of inventory control, with emphasis on exponential smoothing methods. A recent survey by the American Production and Inventory Control Society indicated that the percentage of that Society's membership using exponential smoothing methods in the formulation of sales and demand forecasts had risen from 9% in 1961, through 19% in 1966 to 30% in 1973. At the same time, a decline in the use of subjective forecasting methods such as 'sales manager's estimates' and 'executive opinion' was noticed. Regression techniques are also increasingly being used.

2   Basic trends in demand

In a so-called **stationary** situation, successive values of demand exhibit a random variation about a reasonably steady average. Superimposed on this stationary demand element one might find a **linear growth** element. To expect demand to increase by a fixed amount per month would, of course, be extremely naive; in general, as well as there being random variation in the stationary element of a demand situation, there would also be random variation in the growth element. Over and above the stationary element with superimposed random growth there might also be a **seasonal** element, i.e. for particular months of the year more or less demand compared with an average month's demand would be expected. It is evident that the situation could be yet further complicated by having random variations in the seasonal factors, and in practice other changes not associated with either the linear or seasonal trend can make the real life situation even more complicated.

This discussion indicates how a complicated demand situation can be composed but, in forecasting, the problem is that data already exist. What one wishes to establish is which underlying models might best explain those particular data. Hence, the process of forecasting is essentially one of decomposing existing data values into certain model types (such as those linear or seasonal characteristics) whose parameters can be estimated.

These models are then used to make forecasts of likely future values.

In the next three sections we shall examine ways of forecasting the average demand and the variability of demand in a stationary situation. Section 6 discusses the problem of dealing with trends in a non-stationary situation. The next section outlines a method of monitoring forecasts, in order to identify when a forecasting system breaks down because the underlying demand situation has changed. The final two sections discuss under what circumstances it is worth forecasting and what type of method is most appropriate.

3 Forecasting average demand in a stationary situation

If demand remains fairly steady over a reasonably long period of time, an obvious approach to estimating average demand is to take an arithmetic average of the last n periods of demand data; this is called a **moving average**. If d_t denotes the observed value of demand in period t, then the moving average in period t is defined as

$$m_t = \frac{1}{n} \{d_t + d_{t-1} + \ldots + d_{t-n+1}\}$$

$$= \frac{1}{n} \sum_{i=t}^{t-n+1} d_i$$

This value of m_t is used as a forecast of demand in period $t + 1$.

Such a moving average, although simple in concept, has several major disadvantages when used for forecasting purposes. These disadvantages are:

(a)   When starting a moving average, at least n items of demand data are required.

(b)   The most recent $n - 1$ values of demand data must always be stored for further forecasts to be made. As any average based on less than about a dozen values tends to be too sensitive for forecasting purposes, when forecasts based on twelve or more data periods are made for many items (as is generally the case in manufacturing organisations) the amount of accumulated data storage becomes prohibitive.

(c) The sensitivity of a moving average is inversely proportional to the number of data values included in the average. It is relatively simple to increase the sensitivity by reducing the number of periods incorporated and thus discarding demand data. However, in order to decrease the sensitivity, the number of periods must be increased and very seldom will the demand data be available for long-past time periods.

(d) With a moving average, all data included within the average are equally weighted by $1/n$. In most forecasting situations, with some specific exceptions, demand data can be assumed to become less relevant as they grow older. For forecasting purposes, therefore, one generally requires an average which gives greater weight to more recent observations.

4   Exponential smoothing methods

Most of the disadvantages of the moving average can be over come by using weights which decrease with time. Because, for mathematically true average, the sum of weights must be unity what is ideally required is an infinite series of weights with decreasing values which converge at infinity to produce a total sum of one. Such a series is the exponential series with successive weights

$$\alpha, \alpha(1 - \alpha), \alpha(1 - \alpha)^2, \alpha(1 - \alpha)^3, \ldots$$

which sum to one at infinity if α lies between zero and one. Choosing a value of 0.2, the first seven values of such a series would be

0.200, 0.160, 0.128, 0.102, 0.082, 0.066, 0.052

which sum to 0.79; it is apparent that if sufficient values are taken, the sum will be near enough one.

Incorporating the exponential series as the weighting series yields an **exponentially weighted average** (u_t) defined by

$$u_t = \alpha d_t + \alpha(1 - \alpha)d_{t-1} + \alpha(1 - \alpha)^2 d_{t-2}$$
$$+ \alpha(1 - \alpha)^3 d_{t-3} + \ldots$$

or

$$u_t = \alpha d_t + (1 - \alpha)[\alpha d_{t-1} + \alpha(1 - \alpha)d_{t-2} + (1 - \alpha)^2 d_{t-2}$$
$$+ \ldots]$$

Since the term in square brackets is precisely u_{t-1}, the exponentially weighted average can be rewritten very simply as

$$u_t = \alpha d_t + (1 - \alpha)u_{t-1}$$

As before, u_t is used as a forecast for period $t + 1$. A numerical illustration is given in the first five rows of table 1.

It is apparent that the exponentially weighted average overcomes the problem of storing data (since all previous data are neatly compacted into a single figure represented by u_{t-1}) and the problem of starting up with no previous data (since, once an initial guess for u_{t-1} is made, when fresh data, d_t, arrive the next forecast can be directly evaluated). The sensitivity of the forecast can be changed at any time, simply by changing the value of α, which is known as the **exponential smoothing constant**. This is typically chosen from a range of values between 0.05 and 0.3; the values of 0.1 and 0.2 are the most used.

In the stationary demand situations, because no growth or seasonality is assumed, the forecast for any month in the future is the same as for one month ahead. It is accepted, of course, that the further ahead that forecast is made the wider will be the possible range of demand values that could be expected to fall either side of that average value.

An alternative method of calculating the exponentially weighted average is to re-organise the original equation into the form

$$u_t = u_{t-1} + \alpha(d_t - u_{t-1})$$

In this form the forecast can be evaluated graphically by saying that the new forecast u_t will be equal to the old forecast u_{t-1} plus one-fifth (with $\alpha = 0.2$) of the gap between the old forecast and the current demand value. This procedure is shown for a set of random demand values in figure 1. The gap

Table 1   Fully expanded forecasting schedule for smoothing constant $\alpha =$

		Jan.	Feb.
This month's demand	d_t	60	70
Last month's forecast for this month	u_{t-1}	70.00*	68.0
$\alpha \times$ this month's demand	αd_t	12	14
$(1-\alpha) \times$ last month's forecast for this month	$(1-\alpha)u_{t-1}$	56.0	54.4
This month's forecast for next month	$u_t = \alpha d_t + (1-\alpha)u_{t-1}$	68.0	68.4
This month's forecasting error	$e_t = d_t - u_{t-1}$	-10.0	2.0
$\alpha \times$ absolute value of this month's forecasting error	$\alpha\,|e_t|$	2.0	0.40
$(1-\alpha) \times$ last month's mean absolute deviation	$(1-\alpha)\mathrm{MAD}_{t-1}$	10.00*	9.60
This month's mean absolute deviation	$\mathrm{MAD}_t = \alpha|e_t| + (1-\alpha)\mathrm{MAD}_{t-1}$	12.00	10.00*
This month's estimate of standard deviation	$\sigma_t = 1.25\,\mathrm{MAD}_t$	15.0	12.5
$\alpha \times$ this month's forecasting error	αe_t	-2.0	0.4
$(1-\alpha) \times$ last month's smoothed error	$(1-\alpha)\bar{e}_{t-1}$	1.00*	-0.80
This month's smoothed error	$\bar{e}_t = \alpha e_t + (1-\alpha)\bar{e}_{t-1}$	-1.00	-0.40
Trigg's tracking signal	$T_t = \bar{e}_t/\mathrm{MAD}_t$	-0.08	-0.04

*Items marked with an asterisk * are assumed to be obtained from estimated values in

il	May	June	July	Aug.	Sept.	Oct.	Nov.	Dec.	Jan.
	90	65	70	75	60	80	90	100	95
	68.6	72.9	71.3	71.0	71.8	69.4	71.6	75.2	80.2
	18	13	14	15	12	16	18	20	19
	54.9	58.3	57.0	56.8	57.4	56.6	57.2	60.2	64.2
	72.9	71.3	71.0	71.8	69.4	71.6	75.2	80.2	83.2
	21.4	-7.9	-1.3	4.0	-11.8	10.6	18.4	24.8	14.8
5	4.28	1.57	0.25	0.79	2.36	2.11	3.69	4.95	2.96
4	9.11	10.71	9.82	8.05	7.07	7.54	7.72	9.12	11.25
9	13.39	12.28	10.07	8.84	9.43	9.65	11.41	14.07	14.21
l	16.7	15.3	12.6	11.0	11.8	12.1	14.3	17.6	17.7
5	4.28	-1.57	-0.25	-0.79	-2.36	2.11	3.69	4.95	2.96
0	0.36	3.71	1.71	1.16	1.56	-0.64	1.17	3.88	7.06
5	4.64	2.14	1.46	1.95	-0.80	1.47	4.86	8.83	10.02
3	0.34	0.17	0.14	0.22	-0.08	0.15	0.42	0.62	0.70

:ember of the previous year: $u_{t-1} = 70$, $\bar{e}_{t-1} = 1.25$, $MAD_{t-1} = 12.5$.

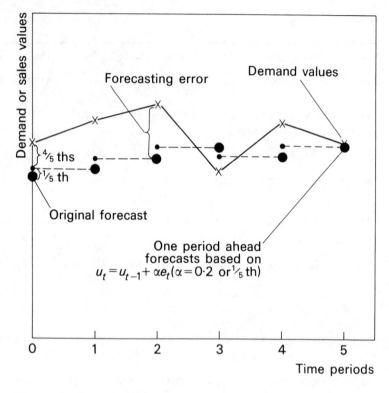

Figure 1. Graphical construction of forecasts based on an exponentially weighted average

$(d_t - u_{t-1})$ is in fact the current value of the **forecasting error** denoted e_t. The previous equation can therefore be rewritten

$$u_t = u_{t-1} + \alpha e_t$$

The forecasting error is calculated in the sixth row of table 1.

5   Calculation of the standard deviation of demand

Examination of figure 2 reveals that, although the average demand has remained at approximately 100 units over the whole year, after June a distinct change in the pattern of

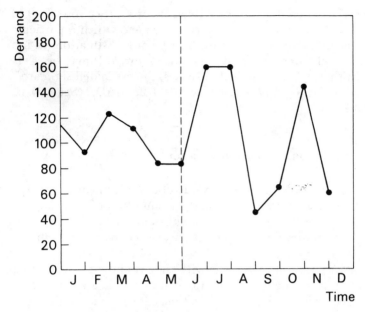

Figure 2. Change in the spread of demand about a
steady average value

demand has occurred. It is apparent that it is the spread of
demand values about the average which has changed significantly
rather than the average level of demand itself. Such a change
would not be detected in a change in the forecast and could,
therefore, only be detected by a separate measure of 'spread'.

The statistic most used in short-term forecasting to measure
spread is known as the **mean absolute deviation** (MAD). As its
name indicates, the mean absolute deviation is simply the mean
or average of the absolute values of errors or deviation from
the long-term average level of demand. With the present forecasting model, the mean absolute deviation for period t can be
calculated as the exponentially weighted average of the absolute
value of forecasting errors

$$\text{MAD}_t = \alpha \mid e_t \mid + \alpha(1 - \alpha) \mid e_{t-1} \mid + \alpha(1 - \alpha)^2 \mid e_{t-2} \mid + \dots$$

which simplifies as before to:

$$\text{MAD}_t = \alpha \mid e_t \mid + (1 - \alpha)\text{MAD}_{t-1}$$

where $|e_t|$ denotes the absolute value of e_t. (See rows 7—9 of table 1.) A measure of variability of demand which is particularly useful in analysing the inventory control situation (as in the next two chapters) is the standard deviation σ. It may be shown that, for all practical purposes, the estimated standard deviation for period t is given by $\sigma_t = 1.25\ \text{MAD}_t$. (See row 10 of table 1.)

6   Non-stationary demand situation

Where the average demand value does not remain relatively constant over a period of time, the assumption of a stationary demand process can no longer be substantiated and forecasts based on the simple exponentially weighted average are no longer appropriate.

The variation of an average with time is known as a **trend** and such trends in a demand situation can vary in character and type. As mentioned in section 2, the character of a trend may be **linear** (either increasing or decreasing over time) or **seasonal** (varying in some cyclical fashion, often yearly). The chief types of trends are additive and multiplicative. An **additive** type of trend is one in which a regular amount is added to or subtracted from each consecutive average demand value. A **multiplicative** (or ratio or exponential) type of trend is subject to a regular *percentage* increase or decrease. Of course, one may have trends exhibiting combinations of these basic characters and types.

Why such different types of trends occur can sometimes be associated with distinct features of demand or marketing situations. If a company is either holding its own proportion of an expanding market or increasing its share of a static market, one would expect its growth in demand to be additive. Only if the company were in the fortunate position of increasing its market share of an overall market which was itself expanding, would one expect the growth type to be multiplicative. In practice, it is usually assumed that trends are of an additive type unless they are obviously multiplicative.

When describing any demand trend, it is necessary to describe both its type and character. Mathematical models have been developed for all the various combinations of character and types of trends described here. However, because of the mathematical complexity of these models, the detailed description of methods for handling non-stationary demand situations lies beyond the scope of this book. The methods are fully described in Lewis[5] (pp. 31–42), including such techniques as Brown's double smoothing method and the Holt-Winters deseasonalising method.

7   Monitoring forecasting systems: Trigg's smoothed error method

Once any routine system for making forecasts has been set up, it is necessary to have some form of monitoring method to indicate when demand becomes so different from the level expected that the forecasting system breaks down. All forecasts are delayed in their response to sudden changes, and the resultant lags brought about by such delays naturally produce larger than usual forecasting errors.

Once a monitoring method has indicated a lack of control in forecasting, questions can be asked as to what is responsible for this sudden change, whether the change is likely to be sustained or not, and if not when is it likely to end. Such information obviously cannot be derived from the forecasting system itself; it is in this type of situation that the market intelligence of the company's salesforce may give useful clues.

The monitoring method proposed in 1964 by Trigg[6] is based on the definition of a **tracking signal** whose value indicates, with specified degrees of statistical confidence, the failure of a forecasting system because of a change in the demand pattern.

Define the **smoothed error**, $\bar{e}_t$, in period t as the exponentially weighted average of forecasting errors in previous periods:

$$\bar{e}_t = \alpha e_t + \alpha(1 - \alpha)e_{t-1} + \ldots$$
$$= \alpha e_t + (1 - \alpha)\bar{e}_{t-1}$$

Trigg's tracking signal for period t (denoted T_t) is defined as the ratio of the exponentially smoothed error to the mean absolute deviation:

$$T_t = \bar{e}_t/\mathrm{MAD}_t$$

Table 2   Tracking signal confidence levels ($\alpha = 0.2$)

Level of confidence (i.e. cumulative probability)	Absolute value of Trigg's tracking signal $\mid T_t \mid$ ($\alpha = 0.2$)
80%	0.54
90%	0.66
95%	0.74
98%	0.81
100%	1.00

This tracking signal ranges between +1 and −1; the higher its absolute value, the more likely it is that the forecasting model is out of control because of a sudden jump in demand. Table 2 gives statistical confidence levels for various values of the tracking signal, on the assumption that the value of the smoothing constant α is 0.2. Thus, if the calculated value of Trigg's tracking signal becomes larger than 0.74, this would indicate with 95% confidence that the forecasting system was out of control.

Now refer back to rows 11−14 of table 1, which present calculations of smoothed errors and tracking signals for the twelve month period. The low absolute value of the tracking signal in March, April and May (0.28, 0.03, 0.34) does not suggest that the jumps in demand from 55 in March to 80 in April to 90 in May (top line) represent a fundamental change in demand. However, because the tracking signal rises to 0.70 in the final period, this confirms with about 94% confidence that the four successive high values of demand of 80, 90, 100 and 95 from October onwards do represent a genuine or significant change in underlying conditions of demand.

When initially starting the calculations for the tracking signal, it is essential to provide reasonable numbers for the immediate past values of the mean absolute deviation (MAD_{t-1}) and, to a lesser extent, the smoothed error ($\bar{e}_{t-1}$). Without such **initialisation** the first tracking signal will be either +1 or −1, indicating to all eagerly awaiting the first computer printout that everything is totally out of control! A reasonable working assumption for initialising these variables is to set MAD_{t-1} equal to one tenth of the initial forecast estimate u_{t-1} and $\bar{e}_{t-1}$ equal to one fiftieth.

A fairly obvious method of using the tracking signal concept in monitoring the stability of forecasts for many products would be simply to highlight those items whose tracking signal exceeded a value of say 0.70. This rather naive approach is unfortunately embodied in much of the computer software in this area. It may highlight as out of control a wildly varying number of items each time an analysis is made. This is not usually very helpful for the investigating team which is trying to find the reasons why certain forecasts have gone out of control and which is attempting to get the forecasts back in control. (The reasons might be a competitor's strike temporarily reducing market competition and thus creating a sudden surge in sales, or alternatively a sales promotion having the same effect.) What such a team requires is a system which highlights a fixed number of items.

Finally, mention should be made of **adaptive forecasting**, the term used for forecasting methods which adapt themselves to the nature of the demand information with which they are dealing. The basic requirement of any such adaptive forecasting method is that as the demand data become relatively more changeable, so the forecast itself responds and becomes more sensitive. Conversely, as the demand becomes relatively more stable , so the forecast becomes less sensitive in order to filter out extraneous 'noise'. In technical terms, this requires that the value of the exponential weighting constant should increase as demand data become more changeable and should decrease as demand becomes more stable. There are various different methods of adaptive forecasting, but description of them is beyond the scope of this book. (See reference 7 and question 4 at the end of this chapter.)

8   Grouping methods: Pareto or ABC analysis

The methods so far described can be invaluable where it is important to obtain regular and up-to-date forecasts of demand, but it would be foolish to spend time and energy applying them to unimportant or slow-moving products. It is, therefore, worth-

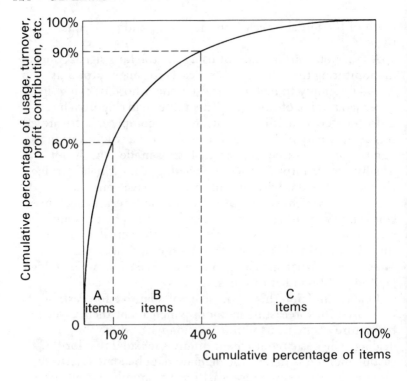

Figure 3. Pareto distribution for stocked items

while classifying a firm's products into several different groups and examining what kind of forecasting system (if any) is most appropriate for the products of each group.

In most industrial organisations a few items represent a large proportion of annual usage value: turnover, profit, invested capital or some other indicator of "importance"; in fact, the distribution of items follows a **Pareto distribution**, as illustrated in figure 3.

The particular shape of a company's Pareto curve can vary in detail depending on the type of organisation being studied, but as a general rule it can be said that approximately:

the first 10% of the stocked items represent 60% of the usage value: these items are termed 'A' items;

the next 30% of the stocked items represent 30% of the usage value: these are termed 'B' items;

the remaining 60% of stocked items represent only 10% of the usage value: these are termed 'C' items.

The division of an organisation's stockholding into three such groups is known as Pareto or ABC analysis. We now discuss the most appropriate forecasting method for each group.

9   Choice of forecasting methods

Category A items. These are expensive or much used items, usually excluding engineering spares for which separate treatment is more appropriate.

With this category of item it will generally be advisable to monitor forecasts so as to identify rapidly changes in the demand pattern. Instigating a monitoring scheme for 'A' items is also reasonably practical because relatively few items are involved. The use of a monitoring scheme will generally preclude the use of adaptive forecasting methods of the Trigg/ Leach adaptive response rate type and thus a non-adaptive forecasting system will normally be adopted. The choice between non-adaptive methods will generally be centred around the fact that the more comprehensive the forecast, the more accurate the results, but the higher the cost of implementation.

Category B items. These are medium cost or moderately used items. As category 'B' items are marginally less costly and less important than 'A' items a rapid response of the forecast to sudden changes in the demand pattern is marginally more important than a sure identification of that change using a monitoring method. Thus an adaptive forecasting method of the Trigg/Leach adaptive response rate type would generally be most suitable. Also with this type of item there is less chance that short-term mathematical forecasts will be 'modified' in the light of sales and market intelligence and, hence, obtaining more responsive forecasts will be well worthwhile. With 'A' items, such is their importance that a certain degree of manual intervention will always take place with the mathematically forecast figures and this feature would nullify the particular advantages of an adaptive type of forecasting method.

Category C items. These are low cost items or "small runners". Because this category represents a large number of stocked items of low usage value, it is usually inadvisable to operate a formalised forecasting scheme, simply because of the high implementation cost involved. Such items are often controlled by a two-bin inventory system (explained in the next chapter) and, because of their cheapness, relative over-stocking can frequently be permitted in order to insulate against any significant variations in demand. Because many 'C' items are standard, and hence rapidly available from several suppliers, it may not be necessary even to take this precaution. It is, therefore, not usual to have a formalised system of forecasting for C items. Rough annual assessment of demand is usually sufficient.

References and further reading

1   Brown R. G., *Statistical Forecasting for Inventory Control*, McGraw-Hill 1959.

2   Brown R. C., *Smoothing, Forecasting and Prediction of Discrete Time Series*, Prentice-Hall 1962.

3   ICI, *Short-term Forecasting*, ICI Monograph No. 2, Oliver and Boyd 1964.

4   ICI, *Cumulative Sum Techniques*, ICI Monograph No. 3, Oliver and Boyd 1964.

5   Lewis C. D., *Demand Analysis and Inventory Control*, Saxon House 1975.

6   Trigg D. W., 'Monitoring a forecasting system', *Operational Research Quarterly*, vol. 15, 1964.

7   Trigg D. W. and Leach A. G., 'Exponential smoothing with adaptive response rate', *Operational Research Quarterly*, vol. 18, 1967.

8   Winter P. R., 'Forecasting sales by exponentially weighted moving averages', *Management Science*, vol. 6, 1960.

Exercises

1   Plot on a piece of graph paper successive demand values of 60, 70, 65, 75, 75, 60, 75, 65, 70, 77 and 60. Using an initial

forecast of 30 for what turned out to be a demand value of 60, plot the succession of forecasts based on a simple exponentially weighted average with a smoothing constant of 0.2. (Use the graphical method illustrated in figure 1.) What conclusions do you draw from the resulting graph as to the length of time a forecast based on a simple exponentially weighted average takes to respond to either a bad initial guess or a sudden jump in demand?

2   Using the attached worksheet (Appendix 2), ignoring rows 4, 5, 6, calculate the smoothed error $\bar{e}_t$ the MAD_t and the tracking signal T_t for the same situation as described in question 1. Does the tracking signal indicate that the forecasting system is out of control?

3   Using rows 4, 5 and 6 of the attached worksheet (Appendix 2) calculate the cumulative sum of squared errors for different values of α from 0.1 up to 0.5 in 0.1 intervals. What value of α do you think produces the best forecast?

4   An adaptive response forecast may be obtained by setting the exponential smoothing constant α equal to the absolute value $|T_t|$ of the tracking signal. Use the attached worksheet to calculate this forecast, and compare it with the simple exponential smoothing method.

11
Inventory Control

C D LEWIS

1 Introduction

Inventory control is the science-based art of ensuring that just enough inventory (or stock) is held by an organisation to meet economically both its internal and external demand commitments. There can be disadvantages in holding either too much or too little inventory; inventory control is primarily concerned with obtaining the correct balance or compromise between these two extremes.

In 1974, the total UK investment in stock was valued at about £14,000m. The different types of stock, and the purposes for which they are held, are as follows.

(a) **Raw material stocks** (represents about 35% of UK total)
By holding stocks of raw material, an organisation decouples its primary production sections or processes (e.g. machine shops and press shops) from its raw material manufacturers or stockists. This allows primary production to be initiated in a shorter period of time than the raw material supplier's delivery time.

(b) **Work-in-progress or stocks-in-process** (about 38%)
The holding of both raw material stocks and stocks of finished goods is generally a planned activity, whereas in-process stocks are likely to exist in any manufacturing organisation whether or not they are planned for. The decoupling

function provided by this category of inventory is to buffer the demand of a later stage in the production process (e.g. sub-assemblies and final assemblies) from the supply of an earlier stage (e.g. machine shops and press shops); this facility is essential for any production process. Without such decoupling all manufacturing stages would need to be perfectly synchronised — a practical impossibility.

(c) **Finished goods** (about 27%)

The stocking of finished goods provides a buffer between the customer demand and the manufacturer's supply. In many cases, because the size of orders required by customers are much less than those supplied by the manufacturer, a wholesaler or stockist can act as intermediary.

We shall begin by describing the two basic inventory control policies, then discuss the costs and usage patterns which determine the design of an appropriate control system.

2   Inventory policies

An organisation's stockholding policy is implemented by a series of rules which determine how and when certain decisions concerning the holding of stocks should be made. This series of rules is known as an **inventory policy.**

There are two basic types of inventory policies. Those in which decisions concerning replenishment are based on the level of inventory held are known as **re-order level** policies and those in which such decisions are made on a regular time basis are known as **re-order cycle** or **periodic review** policies.

(a) **Re-order level policy**   An order for replenishment is placed when the **stock on hand** equals or falls below a fixed value M known as the **re-order level**. Stock on hand includes the stock actually held in stores plus any outstanding replenishment orders less and demand orders which have already been committed to the production programme. In this policy, therefore, the amount of inventory held must be reviewed continuously.

When a replenishment order is placed within a re-order level policy, it is generally for a fixed quantity. A typical example of

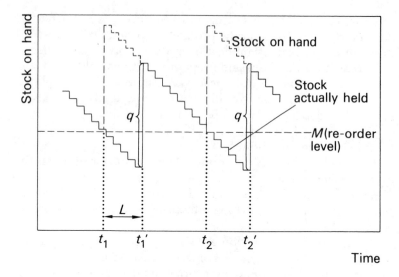

Figure 1. The re-order level policy

inventory balances for a re-order level policy is shown in figure 1. The solid line in this diagram represents the inventory actually held, the broken line is the stock on hand (actual stock plus outstanding replenishments less committed stock). When the re-order level M is broken, a replenishment order of size q is placed but there is a delay before the order actually arrives; this delay is known as the **lead time** (L). In each case, the stock on hand immediately rises by q (since the moment the order is placed it is technically outstanding) but the actual stock continues to be depleted by successive demand withdrawals until the lead time expires and the replenishment order is received at time t_1'. The process is repeated as soon as stock on hand again falls to re-order level M at time t_2.

The excess of the re-order level over the expected demand during the lead time is called the **safety stock** or **buffer stock** (B). If the buffer stock is exhausted, then **back-ordering** may be permitted, whereby demand orders are accepted even when no actual stock remains, thus in effect allowing negative stock to build up.

The most common practical implementation of the re-order

level policy is known as the **two-bin system**. Two bins of the stocked item are kept and a replenishment order is placed when the first bin becomes empty. Further stock is then withdrawn from the second bin until the replenishment order is received to refill the second bin, the remainder being placed in the first bin. The amount of stock held in the second bin, therefore, represents the size of the re-order level. In practice, of course, it is not always necessary to have two separate bins to operate this system; for instance a single bin with a dividing layer or partition serves exactly the same purpose. Some retailers operate by placing a 're-order now' card at an appropriate place in the stock of each item on the counter. However, this single- or two-bin adaptation of the method cannot be used for items that deteriorate or for items which for some reason must be controlled with a first-in, first-out policy.

The single- or two-bin system operates most successfully with physically small items such as nuts, bolts, washers, etc., where committed demand orders are not generally allowed and usually only one outstanding replenishment exists at any time. The system obviously becomes impracticable when large items such as castings and sub-assemblies are involved, where space occupied does not necessarily represent number stored. To be really cheap and effective as a means of controlling stocks, the two-bin system is operated without any formal stock recording, and even auditors are now taking sample estimates of overall stock levels as evidence for audit assessment.

(b) **The re-order cycle or periodic review policy**   The stock on hand is reviewed at fixed periods of time (R), and a replenishment order placed at every review. However, unlike the policy previously described, the size of a replenishment order is variable. This variable replenishment quantity is calculated as that amount of stock which, if there were no lead time, would bring the stock on hand up to some fixed maximum stock level, S. Thus, the size of the replenishment order is equal to S less the stock on hand, and can be different at every review. This replenishment policy ensures that when the level of stock on hand is high at review, a smaller sized replenishment order is placed than when it is low. This can be quite clearly seen in figure 2 which shows a typical stock situation when operating

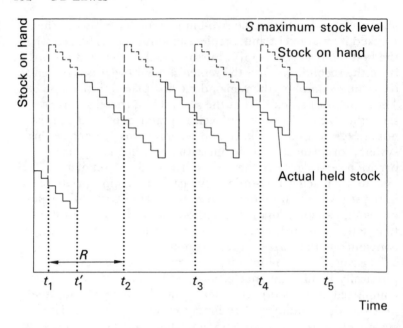

Figure 2. The re-order cycle policy

a re-order cycle policy. Orders are placed at time t_1, t_2, t_3, which are a fixed time R apart; the first order arrives at time t_1'. In the example shown the lead times also vary.

The essential differences between the two inventory policies is that the re-order level policy is one of continuous review, and the operating system must allow replenishment orders to be placed at any time, rather than to be planned in advance as with the re-order cycle policy. One of the principle advantages of planned replenishment is that a single order can be raised to cover many replenishments being placed with a common supplier, thus considerably reducing the cost per replenishment. This advantage is offset by the fact that cyclical policies in general require higher average levels of stock in order to offer similar levels of service (one possible definition of the level of service being the probability of meeting demand 'off the shelf'.)

A domestic comparison can be drawn between the situations of working and non-working wives. The non-working wife, who has the opportunity to shop on any day and knows that her family consumes a maximum of ½ lb of butter per day, might operate a re-order level policy with a re-order level of ½ lb. Her stock holding costs based on an average ½ lb of butter would be very low, but against this she would incur high replenishment costs plus the lost opportunity cost of not working. By contrast, in this same situation, a working wife with the opportunity of shopping only on Saturdays would be forced to operate a cyclical policy such that on each Saturday she would replenish up to 7 x ½ = 3½ lbs of butter to ensure supplies to the following Saturday. Her storage cost would be relatively high (based on an average stock holding of 1¾ lbs of butter) but her replenishment costs very low (based on a single replenishment per week).

3   Inventory operating costs

There are three principle costs involved in operating an inventory system, namely the cost of ordering stock (C_0), the cost of holding stock (C_h) generally given as a percentage (i) of the stock's value (C_m), and the cost of running out of stock (C_s). We shall discuss these in turn.

(a) **Ordering costs** (C_0) (i) All purchase department costs (which usually includes a healthy proportion of an organisation's telephone bill) could be included as part of the ordering cost if replenishment orders are obtained from outside. Such costs are usually apportioned across all stock items ordered through the department, so that the cost of ordering is generally assumed to be the same for all items irrespective of their value. Where replenishment orders are obtained within the organisation the cost of ordering should include the cost of implementing the work's order and also any set-up cost that might be involved.

(ii) For purchased-out items, the cost of receiving goods (which should include any transport costs) might be included in the ordering costs. Again, these are usually allocated on an apportionment basis.

(iii) Those quality control costs incurred as a result of checking received replenishment orders might be included in the cost of ordering, but rarely are, as these costs are absorbed as general overheads.

(iv) Where replenishment orders for purchased-out items are overdue or where internally manufactured items are behind schedule, the cost of 'chasing' or 'expediting' such overdue orders should be included in the cost of ordering.

At current UK prices in 1976 a manufacturer's order cost of less than £10 is unrealistic, which highlights the advantages of multiple replenishment orders. High order costs also explain why manufacturing organisations stipulate minimum quantities below which they are not prepared to trade and why cheaper prices are quoted for cash transactions which can bypass much of the invoicing procedures and their associated costs.

(b) Holding or storage costs (iC_m) C_m is the works prime cost of the stocked item (materials + labour + overheads or, perhaps more simply, materials + value added, but not including profit). Holding cost is expressed as a percentage, i, of prime cost, where i is normally of the order of 25% and is made up as follows:

(i)   the opportunity cost of capital invested in stock. This is usually taken to be the existing rate of interest encountered in obtaining capital from the company's normal sources or the rate of return the company estimates it could obtain by investing capital elsewhere, and has traditionally been of the order of 10%–15% (but see following note).

(ii)   all costs directly associated with storing goods, i.e. storemen's wages, rates, heating and lighting, store's transport, racking and palletisation, protective clothing, weighing equipment, etc. (2%–6%).

(iii)   deterioration costs, including the costs incurred in preventing deterioration (1%–4%).

(iv)   obsolescence costs, including possible rework or scrapping (4%–7%).

(v)   fire and general insurance (1½%).

The above figures give a range for i between 17½% and 34½%; the median of 26% represents ½p in the £ per week.

Note: Until recently the effect of inflation on the prices of goods has not been regarded as an important enough feature to be included in the holding interest rate. However, with price inflation rates now at levels of 12% p.a. or so, it is very debatable whether this ignoring of the effects of inflation should continue. In principle, the expected rate of increase in stock prices should be deducted from the cost of holding stock, thereby promoting a tendency to build up stocks by 'buying now rather than later'. However, such a policy requires a further cash investment and such 'spare' cash is not generally available in times of inflation, especially since interest rates will tend to increase to reflect inflation (though not completely).

(c) Stockout or runout costs (C_s)   These costs are most difficult to assess and to incorporate in mathematical inventory models, since they depend upon such imponderables as loss of customer goodwill, reduction in future orders, change in market share, etc. For this reason, stockout costs are frequently not computed in practice, and are generally only incorporated in the more sophisticated mathematical inventory models which are beyond the scope of this book. Instead, attention is focused on the level of service provided, without trying directly to evaluate that service. Of course, the cost of providing any service level indirectly implies a valuation of that service.

4   Service levels

The efficiency of any stock control policy is indicated by the **level of service** it offers to potential or existing customers in terms of providing stock 'off the shelf' or 'ex-stock'. Opinions as to which definition of service is best have varied widely, but the two most commonly used definitions are 'the probability of not running out of stock' and the 'proportion of annual demand met ex-stock'.

The probability of not running out of stock, as a measure of the effectiveness of a stock control system, has the advantage of being calculated fairly easily but suffers from the disadvantage that it can also be misinterpreted very easily. A 95% probability of not running out of stock strictly interpreted means that, on average, for every 100 replenishment orders placed by the stockholder for his own replenishment, on 95 occasions customer demand will be met ex-stock before the replenishment order is received. On five occasions per 100, therefore, stockouts do occur before the replenishment order is received.

From the customer's point of view, the probability of not running out of stock does not indicate how frequently the holder of stock will be out of stock (unless the stockholder's frequency of replenishment is known, which is most unlikely, except where the stock is raw material or work in progress, and the 'customer' is in fact another department of the same firm). Moreover, it does not indicate how badly or how long the supplier will be out of stock when a stockout does occur and it certainly does not indicate what proportion of the customer's demand will be met ex-stock. From an even more practical point of view, it also does not cover the situation of part-deliveries, where a customer would be more than satisfied to receive a part-delivery on time and the remainder of the order at a later date.

Because the probability of not running out of stock is easy to calculate, it has been used up to now more than any other definition of service in spite of its many disadvantages, and is the method used by virtually all computer packages. Because (in this author's opinion) the probability of not running out of stock is more an indication of good housekeeping on the part of the supplier or vendor than a meaningful measure of service to the customer, this measure of service will be termed the **vendor service level**.

From the customer's point of view a more useful measure of the service offered by a stock control system is the proportion of demand met ex-stock per annum. Such a measure permits the customer to allow for an expected amount short over a year and to protect himself against it, either by arranging to absorb such a shortfall or by holding a limited amount of stock on his own. As this measure is more useful to the customer, it will be re-ferred to here as the **customer service level**. Because the propor-tion of annual demand met ex-stock (the customer service level) can now, with advances in statistical theory, be calculated relatively easily, and indeed linked with the probability of not running out of stock (the vendor service level), it is increasingly being adopted as the measure of service offered by an inventory system, particularly in the USA.

5   Demand: the link with forecasting

The design of any stock control system requires estimated values of the following three parameters

D, the average demand per unit time,

σ, the standard deviation of demand per unit time, and

L, the lead time.

(If the lead time is variable, one needs also to estimate the mean and standard deviation of the lead time; we shall ignore such complications in this chapter.) The values of D and σ may be obtained from a forecasting model as discussed in the last chapter. It would appear sensible to suppose that these values should be updated every time an analysis of the demand situation produced a new forecast. With computerised inventory control systems this is indeed the general practice but, where a manual system of stock recording is in operation using stock record or bin cards, such substitutions are not easily effected, particularly over a large number of items. It must be accepted that the manual system itself limits the degree of control that can be exercised over stocks, and in such situations it might be expedient to update control parameters in line with forecasts at annual intervals and whenever a significant change in demand occurs (see Chapter 10 section 7).

6   Evaluation of stock control parameters: re-order level policy

The traditional method is to determine, quite separately, the replenishment order size (q) and the re-order level (M). The former is calculated as that size which minimises the total cost of ordering and storing. The latter is obtained by management specifying an appropriate vendor service level (i.e. probability of not running out of stock). It is possible to take into account interactions between q and M, but because of its relative simplicity, the traditional method of separate evaluation will be considered here.

(a) **Economic order quantity**   The replenishment quantity is most usually evaluated on the criterion of minimising total annual inventory operating costs, comprising inventory storage costs plus replenishment ordering costs.

Annual inventory storage costs are given by the percentage i multiplied by the average stock valued at unit cost C_m. The average stock will be the buffer stock (B) plus *half* the order quantity $(q/2)$. Annual storage costs thus total

$$\left(B + \frac{q}{2} \right) iC_m$$

Note that they increase with order size q.

The annual cost of ordering is the cost of placing a single replenishment order (C_0) multiplied by the number of re-plenishments (or cycles) per annum (A/q), where A is the annual demand. Annual order costs thus total $C_0 A/q$. Note that they decrease with order size q.

Combining these two costs, the total cost C of ordering q units each time is:

$$C(q) = \left(B + \frac{q}{2} \right) iC_m + C_0 \frac{A}{q}$$

Setting the derivative with respect to q equal to zero to obtain a minimum yields

$$\frac{dC}{dq} = \frac{iC_m}{2} - \frac{AC_0}{q^2} = 0$$

hence an optimal value

$$q^* = \sqrt{\frac{2AC_0}{iC_m}}.$$

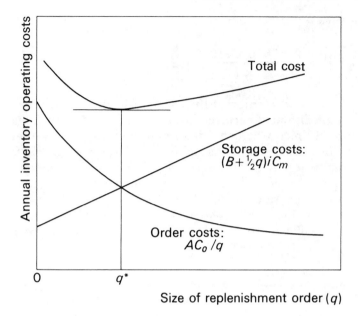

Figure 3. Evaluation of the traditional economic
order quantity

This is the so-called **economic order quantity** (EOQ) which
minimises the cost of operating the present simple inventory
system. A diagrammatic representation is provided in figure 3.
Note that, at the optimum quantity, annual storage costs equal
annual ordering costs.*

To illustrate this, suppose demand (D) averages 100 per week,
totalling 5000 (A) in a 50-week year, Suppose the order cost C_0
is £10, the value of the product C_m is £1 per item and annual
holding costs are 25% of this value. Then economic order

*Geometrically, the derivative represents the slope of the curve, hence the
point where slope is zero is the flat point where total cost is at a minimum.
With storage and replenishment cost functions of the form assumed,
minimum total cost will always be at the quantity where the two component curves intersect. This is not generally the case for the sum of two
curves drawn arbitrarily.

quantity is

$$q^* = \sqrt{\frac{2 \times 5000 \times £10}{0.25 \times £1}} = 632 \text{ items}$$

The above derivation of the economic order quantity assumed that replenishment occurred instantaneously rather than over a period of time. Although this assumption is usually valid for most 'purchased out' items and for some items manufactured internally, it may be necessary to consider what the minimum cost quantity should be in situations where replenishment does occur over a period of time. The relevant replenishment quantity in this situation is the **economic batch quantity** (EBQ) which, using a similar approach to that for developing the economic order quantity, is given by

$$q_b^* = \sqrt{\frac{2AC_0}{iC_m(1 - D/p)}} = q^*\sqrt{\frac{1}{(1 - D/p)}}$$

where p denotes production rate (measured in the same units as demand D). To continue the previous example, if $D = 100$ per week and $p = 300$ per week, then $(1 - D/p) = 2/3$, hence

$$q_b^* = q^*\sqrt{\frac{3}{2}} = 1.225 \times 632 = 774 \text{ items}$$

In many manufacturing situations it is more sensible to express the economic batch quantity in terms of number of weeks of production q_b^*/p. Such values of weeks of production are always rounded to the nearest whole week or to the nearest production planning time unit. In the example, the economic batch quantity involves ordering $774/330 = 2.58$ or 3 weeks' production each time.

The concept of the economic order (or batch) quantity was originally developed as long ago as the 1920's, and the simple square-root formulae shown here have become the parents of a whole family of formulae of ever-increasing complexity. Such formulae have been developed to take into account either (a) that some of the assumptions made in the original model may not be valid in many practical situations, or (b) that the criterion

of minimum cost may not necessarily be the most relevant.
Thus, it has been objected that the basic model takes no account
of stockout costs or price breaks (quantity discounts), that cost
of replenishment may not be independent of order size and that
deviations from the optimum order quantity are not important
because the total cost curve is relatively flat. Alternative criteria
which have been proposed in certain circumstances include
maximum profit per batch, maximum rate of return and minimum cost subject to restrictions on capital, storage space or
set-up costs.

However, from all these theoretical considerations, one
common factor which appears to be generally agreed is that
although the values of individual economic order quantities may
not always be relevant, *the ratio of the value of the economic
order quantity for one stocked item to that of another is always
relevant.* This concept can be shown to be valid by several
different approaches and is also a very useful one as it relates
the size of order quantities between items rather than in isolation. This feature of relative size means that if EOQ's for two
different items come out at 300 units and 100 units, what is of
most importance is that replenishment orders for the first item
should be three times larger than for the second.

(b) Re-order level The re-order level (M) is set equal to the
expected (or average) demand during the lead time plus the
buffer stock (B). The latter is an allowance for occasions when
demand exceeds the average level. It is conveniently expressed
as a specified number (k) of standard deviations of lead time
demand. Assume that demand is normally distributed* with a
mean of D per week (or per month, etc.) and a standard deviation of σ per week. Assume also that demand in any week is
essentially independent of demand in any other week. Then
average demand over L weeks lead time is DL and standard
deviation of lead time demand is $\sigma\sqrt{L}$. The re-order level is
given by

$$M = DL + k\sigma\sqrt{L}$$

*In practice, the normal distribution may not give as accurate a represen-
tation of demand as the lognormal, Poisson, negative exponential or gamma
distributions. Similar formulae and tables are available for these distributions also, but discussion of these is beyond the scope of this book.

The parameter k is called a **standard normal deviate**; evidently, k will be greater the better the vendor service level required. From standard normal distribution tables (see end of book) we can extract information of particular reference to the inventory problem which shows the following relation between k and stockout probability per cycle:

k	Stockout probability per cycle (as % of times a stockout could occur)	Vendor service level (probability of *not* stocking out)
1	15.9%	84.1%
2	2.3%	97.7%
3	0.1%	99.9%

To illustrate this, let demand average D = 100 per week, with a standard deviation of σ = 30 per week, and let lead time be L = 4 weeks. Suppose a vendor service level of 97.7% is required, hence k = 2. Then re-order level is

$$M = (100 \times 4) + (2 \times 30 \sqrt{4}) = 520 \text{ units}$$

Of this amount, 400 units are active stock required to meet average demand during the lead time, and 120 units represent buffer stock (B) to meet above-average demand. The situation is illustrated in figure 4.

In many companies, re-order levels are expressed in terms of weeks (or months, etc.) of average demand rather than in units of stock. Thus a re-order level may be expressed as 'four week's supply' rather than as 400 units. To do this, simply divide the re-order level by the rate of demand, hence

$$\text{re-order level (in time units)} = \frac{M}{D} = L + \frac{k\sigma\sqrt{L}}{D}$$

In the present example, a re-order level of 520 units represents $520/100$ = 5.2 weeks' supply. Too often, however, when this type of definition is used the practice is to make the re-order level simply equal to the average lead time demand. Such a rule of thumb does not take into account more than average demand

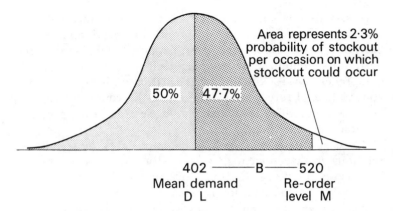

Figure 4. Probability distribution of normal demand during the lead time

and, hence, results in a very low level of vendor service (theoretically only 50%).

It is quite straightforward to relate probability of stockout to expected number of stockouts per year. If A denotes annual demand and q the replenishment order quantity, then there will, on average, be A/q replenishment cycles per year. If P denotes the probability of *not* running out of stock, then the expected number of stockouts per year is $(1 - P)A/q$. For the numerical example just given, where the economic order quantity is $q = 632$ and annual demand is $A = 5000$, there would be 5000/632 or approximately 8 replenishments per year. If the vendor service level is 97.7%, then the average frequency of stockout would be:

$$(1 - 0.977)\frac{5000}{632} = 0.182 \text{ times per year}$$

or approximately once every 5½ years.

7 Categorisation of stocked items

When deciding which type of inventory policy to use for the different types of items held in stock by an organisation, a necessary first step is to group items using some measure or criterion of importance. Having grouped stocked items on a basis of relative importance, it is then possible to use the properties of the method of grouping itself to arrive at an overall comprehensive stocking policy. The situation is exactly analogous to that of forecasting and, in fact, the same approach may be used as described in the concluding section of the previous chapter.

To recapitulate, ABC or Pareto analysis uses the well-known relationship that in virtually all inventory situations a large proportion of an organisation's investment, usage value, turnover, or profit contribution is associated with relatively few items. This general relationship was shown in figure 3 of Chapter 10. Although for different organisations the relationship can vary somewhat, it is still generally true that a few items are of great importance and a large proportion of items are, relatively speaking, unimportant.

Category A items   These are the most important 20% of the items, representing 80% of, say, turnover. It is usual with valuable items such as these (typically three times the average individual value) to try to obtain a high degree of control of stocks. There is a tendency therefore to use inventory control policies of the periodic review type for this category of item. Such policies ensure that the stock position is reviewed regularly, irrespective of demand, whereas in a re-order level type of policy it is the demand situation which determines when reviews take place. In the latter type of policy, if demand is particularly low for a period of time, the frequency at which reviews of the stock situation take place drops significantly compared with the average, and this can be a prime cause of dead stocks being created as items gradually become obsolete.

The pure re-order cycle policy ensures that replenishments are placed regularly at each and every review although the size of the individual replenishment order varies. Such a method of replenishment might fit in well with contract buying.

Category B items   These are the next 15% of the items representing 15% of turnover. For these medium-cost items a re-order level policy is generally most suitable. Where replenishments for several items are obtained from a single source, however, again it may be practical to operate a regular review type of inventory policy to enable several orders to be placed simultaneously, thus reducing ordering and transport costs.

Category C items   These are the large majority of items representing relatively little value. The re-order level of two-bin (or single-bin) policy is usually most appropriate for C items. This method offers a reasonable degree of control with a minimum of record-keeping. If space allows, a degree of overstocking can generally be allowed, simply because of the cheapness of the items involved, in order to reduce the probability of stockouts. Readers are reminded that the two-bin type of policy is not suitable for items that deteriorate as it is essentially a last-in first-out (LIFO) policy rather than a first-in first-out (FIFO) policy. For C items it is not usual to update stock control parameters in line with forecasts, as forecasts will not generally be made for this type of item — annual updating is, therefore, more usual. Often, in fact, this policy is operated with no paper records at all and auditors accept limited sampling as a method of assessing value for audit purposes. This is the case in the company described in the next chapter.

References and further reading

1   Brown R. G., *Decision Rules for Inventory Management*, Holt, Rinehart and Winston 1967.

2   Buchan J. and Koenigsberg E., *Scientific Inventory Management*, Prentice-Hall 1963.

3   ICI, *Problems of Stocks and Storage*, ICI Monograph No 4, Oliver and Boyd 1967.

4   Lewis C. D., *Scientific Inventory Control*, Butterworths 1970.

5   Thomas A., *Stock Control in Manufacturing Industries*, Gower Press 1968.

Exercises

1   What probability of not running out is afforded by a re-order level of 200 units when demand per week is normally

distributed with a mean value of 40 and a standard deviation of 20, if the lead time is fixed at 3 weeks?

2   Calculate the value of the economic order quantity for the situation in which the annual sales turnover is 3000 items, the cost of placing a replenishment order is £10 and the cost of holding an item of stock for a year is £1.50? How low would the order quantity have to be before total inventory operating costs rose by 10%?

3   In a situation where demand per month is distributed normally with an average value of 50 and a standard deviation of 15, what re-order level is required to achieve a vendor service level of 99% if replenishment orders are 200 units and lead time is 4 months?

12

Stock Control in the Welding Industry*

P G FITZGERALD AND M J HARRISON

1   Introduction

This chapter describes a study carried out by a company specialising in the arc welding industry. Its products can be classified as:

(i)   *Machines:* arc welding generators, transformers, rectifiers, arc welding machines, and cutting and gauging equipment;
(ii)   *Spares:* for present and past models;
(iii)   *Accessories:* welders tools, protective clothing, etc.;
(iv)   *Consumables:* electrodes, electrode wires and flux cored wire.

At the start of the work being reported, the company's turnover was of the order of five million pounds and it employed some 500 personnel.

The object of the assignment was to devise a method of *controlling* stocks, rather than simply *recording* them as was done at the time, for the company operated a simple system with few rules loosely applied. The study recommended the immediate implementation of a simple but robust method of manual

*We wish to thank the Company staff for the cooperation they gave to us, and the Managing Director for his commitment to and patience with our efforts.

control. This system provided the necessary preparatory ground-work so that the company would be able to move easily to a more sophisticated and sensitive control system when a computer system was implemented. It also formed an excellent training vehicle for the company staff which should greatly ease the eventual introduction of the more advanced system.

2   Management services: method of working

The company itself is a subsidiary of a large engineering group. The OR division is located within the Group Management Services (GMS) department. GMS operate exclusively on an in-house activity. They form a cost centre which ideally balances its costs on a year by year basis through a time-based charging rate which works out cheaper than any outside agency. In this way, the managing director of a subsidiary company has an incentive to use Group resources, but also tends only to authorise work which he considers of real value.

The Unit Managing Director will agree a project with one of the managers of GMS and then preside over a monthly meeting to discuss a written report on progress to date, which is monitored against a work plan (both in cost and time) submitted as part of the terms of reference. A final report is invariably issued. Problem formulation, analysis and solution are separated from implementation, since in some cases the subsidiary company has the resources for the latter. Implementation nevertheless forms a high percentage of work done.

Within GMS are four divisions: two main general consultant divisions containing both accountants and industrial engineers, an operational research division and a systems division. Most work comes originally to the Service from personal contacts between the Director and managers of GMS on the one hand and the personnel in operating units on the other. In the present case a fairly routine investigation into aspects of accounting initiated by the Managing Director of the Company led to the GMS accountant becoming unhappy with the stock recording and stock control systems. From this in turn came a survey of the problem and then terms of reference for the present study.

Most OR work is done as in this case by a single analyst,

supported by a manager or senior consultant. As often as is possible the analyst works on site, acquiring over the period of the assignment the trust and knowledge of the capabilities of the staff, so that the solution proposed is one that will be used rather than one that is ideal. This is a vital element to success: the process of criticism and change is a painful one for the recipients who need to be *slowly* converted and encouraged over a period (rapid conversions do not last) — and the more mathematics involved, the more faith is required by the user in the analyst whom he must come to trust and respect. Involvement is *the* key to any supporting service.

Supervision is through weekly meetings, by either the OR manager or a senior consultant. In some cases, though not here, managers from other divisions undertake the supervision: this both extends the range of their own expertise and allows a single overall command of several related projects, embracing accountants and industrial engineers as well.

3   Terms of reference

It was agreed that the work would initiallly be restricted to the two categories of machines and spares (though future work would deal with control of accessories and consumables). The work would comprise:

1   a data collection system to allow analysis of usage and of the variable lead times for orders;

2   examination of the rationale behind the six-month machine production plan and recommendations from this;

3   parts explosion plan for the above;

4   the introduction of a simple manual short-term fore-casting system using historical information;

5   the design of a stock control system for both categories covering (a) levels of service (including running out of stock), (b) variable lead times, (c) price breaks;

6   the provision of two solutions: (a) a short-term manual system to last up to 12 months, (b) a preferred solution

dependent on the provision of a computer or computing facilities and with a longer time-scale for implementation. It was anticipated that in both cases control would vary according to some categorisation of items.

7   the application of programmes already developed by the OR Divison for making the most of price breaks in fixing the economic order quantities.

This list of work was scheduled to take 10 person-weeks, a time scale which was in fact achieved.

4   Original system

Each time an item was used, either in production or supplied as a spare, the transaction was recorded on the accounts department's NCR (National Cash Register Co.) stock card, and the outstanding stock balance adjusted. All goods received, whether from outside suppliers or from the company's own production department, were also processed through the system. After each transaction the stock-on-hand was checked against a re-order level value and if the re-order level had been broken, then the part number was printed out at the left-hand side of the backing sheet. These backing sheets were sent to the stock control department each day for action.

The stock control department had a system of shuttle cards on which they recorded details of outstanding orders. They first checked to see if an order had been placed; if one had not, then they considered the item and from experience ordered an appropriate quantity. The existing NCR system did not record details of orders outstanding. As a result, not only were items which had just broken their re-order level marked for attention by the stock control department, but so was every item with an order outstanding. This method of control caused much unnecessary duplication of effort and, more important, the system could result in errors leading to over-stocking or to running out of stock. For example, the staff in the stock control department could become familiar with particular item numbers which had orders outstanding for some time. If, shortly after these outstanding orders were delivered, the re-order level was again broken, then the stock control department could fail to realise that another order was required.

5   Analysis of stock cards

At the start of this assignment it was found that there was very little accurate information available about the stock. For example, it was difficult to find out the annual usage per item or the percentage of items supplied as spares (as against those supplied for machine build) or any information on the distributions of unit standard costs or usage.

Clearly, the first task was to examine in detail a random sample of stock items. In many stock control assignments a

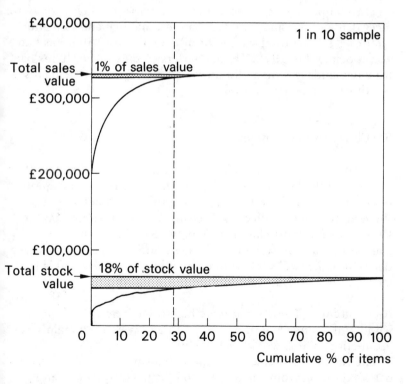

Figure 1. Pareto curves for 1972 stock and sales

sample of 1 in 25 items is sufficient to give a meaningful picture
of the stock. However, in view of the large and disparate range
of items held in stock by the company, it was felt that a 1 in 10
sample would be necessary to obtain an accurate representation.
Data were collected and analysed by computer.

Pareto curves of the kind discussed in Chapters 10 and 11 were
plotted for both sales value and stock value; they are shown super
imposed in figure 1.

The sales ranking analysis shows that 28% of the items
accounted for 99% of total sales value and 72% of total stock
value. In other words, 18% of the stock value (about £11,900)
was held for only 1% of sales value (about £3,300). This stock
was sufficient for an average of 187 weeks' supply. It was
reasonable to assume that there was scope for a reduction in
stock here.

The company asked whether these stocks were held largely to
meet demand for spares rather than internal demand in manufacturing. Of the total sample of 522 items only 165 items had a
spares demand in 1972. Three quarters of these latter items had
total demands less than 100 units and 80% had total demands
worth less than £100 in value.

6   Classification of items

Effective control of stocks does not mean putting equal effort
into the control of all items. The method and hence the amount
of control should be varied according to the characteristics of
the item to be controlled, as discussed in the previous chapter.
Here three different classes of item were defined. The exact
transition point between one class and another is a management
decision which will vary from company to company and is to
some extent arbitrary.

A-class items   These items were high-value items, i.e. items
whose unit standard cost exceeded £3 and were used mainly for
production. These would be scheduled.

The future requirement for these items was determined by a
parts explosion from the production plan. The quantity and
frequency of call-off would depend on the production plan. The

safety stock held for these items was recommended to be one call-off quantity. This could be reduced with experience once the reliability of the supplier had been established. If the item also had a small spares demand, then the call-off quantity could be increased proportionally to cover this additional demand.

B-class items These were items used mainly for spares, but also included those items used for production whose unit standard cost was less than £3. The first requirement for these items was a forecast of demand. The technique of simple exponential smoothing (see Chapter 11) was recommended with a forecast interval of four weeks. The updating of this forecast was carried out by a special programme on the NCR machines. An estimate of lead time was required for each item. (The Appendix to this chapter discusses some problems in the definition of lead time.) An examination of a small sample of shuttle cards showed that in their current form they were not very suitable documents for extracting lead times and, therefore, a simple revision of these shuttle cards was recommended.

The re-order level for B-class items was set at demand in one lead time plus a safety stock of demand in one lead time for those items whose lead time was 10 weeks or less. For items whose lead time was more than 10 weeks, the safety stock would be the demand in half the lead time. When items broke the re-order level, an order for an economic order quantity was generated.

C-class items These were low-value, low-usage items whose value and usage were such that only the simplest control system was worthwhile.

For these items, the Company was strongly urged to discontinue formal recording or usage in favour of a two-bin system. In the past, despite the attractiveness of such a simple method of control, problems had been encountered elsewhere with auditors. The objection had now been overcome: auditors were prepared to accept that the ratio of total stocks in this category to total Company stocks would remain approximately constant, and hence were prepared to derive the value of C-class items from an audit of the classes recorded in full.

The method of operation of a two-bin system would be as

follows:

(a) The physical stock would be divided into two bins and items would be issued from the stores directly. When the first bin was empty, then the stores sent the item number and description to the stock control/buying office so that goods were re-ordered. The stores then used the second bin to supply demand.

(b) The buying office checked the date of the last order and quantity ordered: if it was about six months since the last order was placed then the same quantity was ordered again.

(c) If it had been a much shorter time, then the order quantity was increased to equal approximately six months new demand. It might not be possible to be too precise on quantity ordered as these low value items are frequently sold in fixed size packets.

Using the above definitions of classes, the items were distributed as follows:

	Number	%
Class A items	393	6.3
Class B items	2,568	41.0
Class C items	774	12.4
Manual items	2,513	40.1
Others	12	0.2
	6,260	100

Manual items were those with a past history of demand but with zero usage for the last year. 'Others' were items seen as a specialised requirement considered to be a one-off demand.

7 Proposed manual system

In order to implement the recommendations made in the report, changes had to be made to the NCR stock card system. At that time, outstanding orders were not recorded on the NCR machines. It was an essential first step that all stock cards be modified to accumulate and print out the outstanding order

balance. It was this feature that required expenditure on modifying the NCR hardware and systems. Although the current
system recorded each transaction, no demand statistics were
accumulated. Such statistics were essential for the future and
the cards would now accumulate and store the demand to date.

Before adopting the revised system all re-order levels had to
be checked and if necessary re-calculated. After each transaction
the re-order level was checked against stock on hand, i.e. stock
actually held plus orders outstanding (not just against stock
actually held, as before).

As an additional safeguard against fluctuations in demand or
lead times, a warning level was stored on each card, at half the
safety stock. After each transaction the stock actually held was
compared with the warning level and if it had been broken then
the stock control department would urge delivery of the item.
This method of control directed effort towards those items
most likely to run out of stock at any time, rather than simply
overdue items.

All B-class items were to be analysed every four weeks by a
new programme which calculated a new forecast of demand
using simple exponential smoothing. Using this forecast, the re-
order level and warning level were updated. Stock actually held
and orders outstanding were compared with the revised re-order
and warning levels, and appropriate action taken.

All these proposals were submitted to NCR who submitted
quotations for both the hardware and software modifications
required.

8 Proposed computer system

The manual system just described was a very simple system.
The success of any system depends on the accurate application
of the rules within a prescribed time limit. Hence, if the system
is a manual one, the opportunity for error can be minimised by
keeping the number and complexity of the rules as low as
possible. When one considers a computer system, only the
accuracy of the data has to be considered as the computer has
the ability to apply sophisticated rules rapidly and without error.

A computer system has an additional advantage. One of the

major sources of dissatisfaction in user companies with the performance of stock control systems hinged on the vagaries of the business cycle. As level of activity alters, so the parameters of the system should be changed — items should be shifted from one class to another and re-order quantities should be recalculated. Often a deep understanding of the system in use does not exist at unit level. The system remains unaltered and grows steadily out of date, attracting greater scepticism as to its effectiveness until the day dawns when an informal system is created by user staff, who run their own books to give them what the system no longer can give them. This is one of the real advantages of an adaptive system and explains the need for a computer solution in the longer term.

Scheduled (A-class) items   Recall that these items were to be controlled by a forecast based on a parts explosion of the production plan. When the computerised system is implemented, the stock control of these items should be linked with the production control package, so that any modifications to the production plan result in the immediate review of availability and lead to the reservation of stock and to a review of the outstanding schedules position. At the time of the study it was not possible to give more detailed rules for control since these would depend on the production control system adopted.

B-class items   Many of the B-class items experienced intermittent demand patterns, the individual demands usually being for several items at a time. Many conventional stock control systems involve the use of exponential smoothing techniques. It has been found that over a period of time these systems tend to underestimate the size of individual demands, but to overestimate the long-term average demands. Since the average demand is used in many stock replenishment and batch size formulae, this can result in a high aggregate stock level being generated. A method of controlling this type of item was devised which made separate estimates of demand size and arrival times.

It was recommended that, apart from this revised method of forecasting, a standard method of operation be used for these B-class items. The method would incorporate the following procedures (see Chapter 10):

(a)   re-classification of items at regular intervals;
(b)   monitoring of lead times;
(c)   optimisation of smoothing constant;
(d)   inclusion and revision of a tracking signal;
(e)   half-yearly analysis of stock and sales profiles, particularly relating to spares.

Clearly, it was not necessary or desirable to attempt to specify detailed operational procedures at the time of the study, as much of the detail depended on the type of computer system adopted by the Company.

C-class items   The fundamental decision to be made with these items was whether to include their records in a computerised system. The decision would be strongly influenced by the computer system adopted. The major cost in time and effort would be the initial creation of the additional 3000 computer records. The cost and effort involved in updating these records would not be very great as the expected frequency of movement of these items was low. In the event, it was recommended that the two-bin system be continued.

9   Implementation

A simple computer system was developed based on the manual system design. The reasons for this were:

(a)   costs for the necessary changes to the NCR system were considered unjustified for the short lifetime of the manual system;
(b)   computing resources became available earlier than expected;
(c)   it was desirable that the production staff should gain experience in computer systems as soon as possible.

This system was implemented in May 1975 and by November 1975 stock had been reduced by 27.3%, equivalent to £351,000. Of this sum, the system contributed about one-third to the saving. A further third was saved on the information now produced by the system, available for the first time, e.g. highlighting of overstocking, identification of redundant stock. The remainder was saved by actions that would have been taken in any case.

Appendix: The definition of lead time

There is some controversy concerning the exact definition of lead time. In any situation it is important to be clear about the definition, since different interpretations can give very different results.

Is it the quoted time for delivery given by the supplier? If one takes this as the lead time then one must consider the various philosophies behind quotes given by different suppliers. A particular supplier may give a quote that he knows will be acceptable to the customer at the time to ensure obtaining the business. The same supplier may vary his quote depending on the length of his order book, which in turn is a function of the long-term business cycle. Some suppliers may give standard quotes of ten weeks. The quotes never vary, and while it is possible that they reflect the average lead time achieved by the supplier, they bear no relationship to his present delivery performance. It may be relevant to ask whether a particular supplier is capable of giving or willing to give an accurate quote.

Should the lead time be defined as the time from date of order to date of first delivery? This, of course, applies only to items which are subject to split delivery. If one takes this definition as lead time then one must consider the percentage of the total order supplied on the first delivery and the reason for a split delivery being made. If an item is required urgently and a significant amount of progress chasing is needed, then it is probable that the supplier will try to supply at least part of the order early. It is sometimes argued that since this first delivery gets one out of trouble then this measures the true lead time. However, if one assumes this artificially reduced lead time as the norm, then one is deliberately building into the system a panic situation, since this delivery performance is achieved only by using pressure in the form of progress chasing, a costly extra. There can be no justification for not using a realistic lead time and thus preventing unnecessary panics. Indeed, the great cost of continued chasing reflects on the cost per order of the buying department — a cost which ought to be regularly reviewed and which forms one of the performance criteria for this department.

The definition of lead time that has been adopted in this chapter is the time between the order placed and delivery of 70% of the order. The figure of 70% is to some extent arbitrary but it is important to employ rules which are unambiguous and clearly understood.

A number of practical points can be added:

1   The lead time includes the time taken internally to generate the order. Reducing this makes the company more responsive and also reduces the need for working capital.

2   One of the purposes of the system is anticipation. Proper anticipation gives suppliers a better chance to offer an effective service, it minimises 'panics' — which have the unfortunate effect of frequently setting off emergency actions elsewhere — and generally it reduces the cost of achieving the results necessary.

3   Computerisation offers the opportunity of monitoring the performance of suppliers. This not only enables the company to assess a supplier's likely performance — it also leads over time to an improvement in this performance.

13

Queueing Theory

S C LITTLECHILD

1 Introduction

Everyone has stood in queues at banks, barber shops and bus stops and no doubt agrees that queueing is a nuisance. But how can a theory of queues be developed, and how is it likely to help a manager? A theory is possible because there are usually certain regularities about arrivals and service of customers; these regularities can be described by statistical distributions and the resulting performance of the system can to some extent be deduced by mathematical analysis. Queueing theory is useful because it embraces a much wider range of phenomena than the ones just quoted. It encompasses queues of machines or paper, not just persons, and it extends to the study of delay, whether or not a physical queue is observed. Queueing theory is therefore concerned with problems such as congestion in telephone systems, airports and harbours; machines out of action waiting for repair; stockouts in inventory systems; the design of appointments systems and production schedules, and so on.

Why does delay occur in these systems? Essentially because it is not possible or worthwhile exactly to tailor the supply of the required commodity to the demand for it. This may be because the timing of the demand is uncertain (for instance, one does not know exactly how many customers will arrive at any time of day) or because service can only be provided in 'lumps' (for example, one or two or three cashiers) or because peak demands last for a relatively short time and it is not worth providing extra capacity for them (in telephone systems or at airports).

Delay can be expensive. People standing in queues are precluded from doing more useful work; idle machines are not producing; aircraft circling over airports are burning up fuel; work in progress may be expensive to store; production held up may mean penalty payments or the loss of an order, etc. On the other hand it can be expensive to avoid delay: repairmen must be paid, airport and production capacity costs money. The problem for the managers of these various systems is thus to design the system in such a way that the total costs are minimised (or the total benefits maximised). Costs of providing better service must be weighed against the costs of *not* providing it.

In many cases, an adequate system can be determined by trial and error. For example, a bank manager will soon get to know the usual daily pattern and variation of customers and will work out in his head how many cashiers are appropriate. By contrast, other situations require large and irreversible investments where experimentation would be prohibitively expensive. One cannot design airports, roads and harbours by trial and error; once they have been built to a particular design, one has to live with that decision for many years.

In a wide variety of circumstances, queueing theory may be used to predict how different systems will operate. More precisely, it provides explicit expressions relating the design of the system to the length and frequency of queues, the average waiting time, the probability of no delay at all, etc. By the design of the system is meant the rate of arrival of 'customers', the number and speed of the 'servers' and the arrangements relating customers to servers. For example, simple formulae can be provided to predict how the average time spent queueing at a supermarket would vary with the number of checkout counters operated.

Queueing theory is useful only in a limited number of situations, but in those situations it is used quite intensively. In the early part of this century, pioneering studies were made in telephone engineering by the Danish engineer Erlang (whose name has subsequently been adopted as the standard unit of telephone traffic intensity), and queueing theory still lies at the core of this profession. Another early classic was the evaluation of standards of service at bridge and tunnel toll booths in New York.[3] Queueing theory has also been used to study the maximum sorting capacity of a single clerk at airline ticket counters, where there was a danger that the whole passenger check-in area would have to be re-designed.[6] It was used to predict and compare the performance of different taxiway systems at Heathrow Airport,[10] and to minimise the 'pool' of coaches needed to transport passengers between aircraft and terminals.[4]

Unfortunately, queueing theory can handle only relatively simple situations. Complex situations involving networks of queues (as in many production scheduling systems) or involving frequent human intervention based on the state of the system (for example, the provision of an emergency cashier for a half hour or the switching of men from one task to another or the adjustment of customer arrivals) are beyond the scope of queueing theory (at least, beyond present mathematical results). In these situations one often has recourse to simulation, as described in Chapters 15 and 16.

The difference between simulation and queueing theory is that the former involves the repeated trial of a particular system, under different patterns of customer arrivals or service performance, until one has built up an adequate picture of how the system behaves. Queueing theory gives an explicit picture, generally in the form of a mathematical function or graph, relating behaviour to certain system parameters. In this case, one may see immediately how the system would respond to changes in these parameters, whereas with simulation one would have to repeat a whole exercise. Simulation allows one to test out ideas for different system designs but does not, of itself, lead to a 'best' design. Queueing theory thus has a distinct advantage in the limited number of situations where it can be applied, but simulation is a more flexible technique.

2   Elements of a queueing system

As remarked earlier, the main elements of a queueing system are the **arrival pattern** of the **customers**, the **queue discipline** for customers who cannot be served immediately, and the **service mechanism** itself. We shall briefly examine each of these elements in turn. It should be borne in mind that 'customers' and 'servers' are not necessarily people.

(a) **Arrival of customers**   The arrival pattern may be known, or **deterministic**, as with an appointments system, or it may be uncertain, or **random**, as in a grocery shop. Even with appointments systems the customers are seldom exactly on time, so that actual arrival patterns are unknown. It is generally convenient to describe such arrival patterns by means of **probability distributions** (discussed in more detail in the next section). Customers may arrive **singly** or in **bulk**. The arrival date may be independent of the state of the system, or it may depend upon it — for example, customers may not enter the barber shop if there are several people already waiting (this is called **balking**); the rate at which machines break down will depend upon the rate at which broken machines are mended. Arrival rate may be constant or may vary over time, with peaks and troughs. Customers may be identical or different in relevant respects.

(b) **Queue discipline**   The simplest situation is where the arriving customer joins a single queue until it is his turn to be served. Service may be on a **first-in first-out** (FIFO) basis, or on a **last-in first-out** (LIFO) basis (as often with goods drawn from stock), or even on a **random** basis. Servers may discriminate between different classes of customers (urgent hospital cases, or familiar restaurant patrons, or first-class passengers at airports). Instead of one queue there may be several, as at banks. In this case customers may jump from one queue to another (**jockey**) or they may be constrained to stay in the same queue. There may be **limits on queue size** (for example, because the telephone board cannot record more than a specified number of callers, as described in the next chapter). Some customers may leave the system (or **renege**) if they are not served within a certain period of time.

(c) **Service mechanism**   There may be one or many servers; in the latter case they may be identical or they may differ with regard to the speed at which they work or the type of customers which they handle. The speed of working may be constant or it may vary around a given average rate. Again, it is convenient to use probability distributions to describe the service pattern. The number of servers and the average service rate may depend upon the time of day, or upon the number of customers who have already been served, or upon the number which remain to be served. Different servers may be alternatives for the customer (i.e. they work in **parallel**) or he may have to go through all of them (i.e. they work in **series**). For example, the sequence of operations in joining and trueing a wheel rim, adding, tightening and testing spokes and hub, etc., comprises quite a complex system of interrelated queues in series, where arrival rates at one queue depend upon service rates at another.

Thus, in describing a queueing situation one must specify every detail of the above three elements. Systems which appear to be identical may differ in some apparently small detail which may have significant implications for the way in which the two systems behave. On the other hand, two situations which appear to bear no relation to each other, such as the sorting of airline tickets and the serving of Post Office customers, may well be formally represented by exactly the same model.

3   Description of a simple queueing system

Consider the following simple example. Customers arrive at a self-service grocery shop at an average rate of 24 per hour. There is only one assistant. The time that is taken for the assistant to total up the bill and make change varies with the size of purchase, but the average time is two minutes. Are queues of customers likely to be the exception or the rule? What is the average number of customers waiting to pay? What is the average time spent waiting to pay?

This is one of the simplest kinds of problem which queueing theory can handle. The answers can be obtained from formulae in a matter of seconds, but before we give the answers the reader might like to hazard guesses of his own in order to test his intuition.

It seems reasonable to assume that the system in this example involves a single queue operating on a first-come first-served basis, with no limits on the size of queue, and no balking, reneging or jockeying.

We need to specify a little more closely the arrival and service patterns. Although the average arrival rate is 24 per hour (or 0.4 per minute) this does not mean that one customer arrives every 150 seconds. Five customers may arrive in one five-minute period then ten minutes may elapse before another customer arrives. In principle it is possible to measure how often 0, 1, 2, 3, . . . customers arrive in each interval of, say one minute. In this way one could build up a **frequency distribution**, and measure the **mean** (or **average**) arrival rate and the **variance** or **standard deviation** of the arrival rate.

Let us suppose that customers arrive completely at random, so that (given the average arrival rate) the probability of a customer arriving in any short interval of time, T, depends *only* upon the length of that interval, and *not* upon the time of day or upon the number of customers who have already arrived. In this case it may be shown mathematically that the number of arrivals in any time interval of length T is given by the **Poisson probability distribution**:

$$P\{n \text{ arrivals in time } T\} = \frac{(\lambda T)^n e^{-\lambda T}}{n!} \quad \text{for} \quad n = 0,1,2, \ldots$$

where λ denotes the average arrival rate in time T. In our example, setting $T = 1$ minute and $\lambda = 0.4$ yields

$$P\{n \text{ arrivals in any minute}\} = \frac{0.4^n e^{-0.4}}{n!} \quad \text{for} \quad n = 0,1,2, \ldots$$

These probabilities have been calculated and expressed in tables such as table 1. This shows that, in any given minute, the chances of 0, 1, 2 or 3 customers arriving are 67%, 27%, 5% and 1%, respectively. The chances of 4 or more customers arriving in any minute are negligible.

If customers arrive according to a Poisson distribution with mean λ (per minute), it may be shown mathematically that the probability distribution of time intervals *between* successive arrivals is described by the **negative exponential function**:

$$f(t) = \lambda e^{-\lambda t}$$

which has both mean and standard deviation equal to $1/\lambda$

Table 1 Poisson probabilities: a table of $e^{-\lambda}\lambda^n/n!$

λ	$n=0$	1	2	3	4	5	6	7	8	9	10	11	12
.1	.9048	.0905	.0045	.0002	.0000								
.2	.8187	.1637	.0164	.0011	.0001								
.3	.7408	.2222	.0333	.0033	.0002	.0000							
.4	.6703	.2681	.0536	.0072	.0007	.0001	.0000						
.5	.6065	.3033	.0758	.0126	.0016	.0002	.0000						
.6	.5488	.3293	.0988	.0198	.0030	.0004	.0000						
.7	.4966	.3476	.1217	.0284	.0050	.0007	.0001						
.8	.4493	.3595	.1438	.0383	.0077	.0012	.0002	.0000					
.9	.4066	.3659	.1647	.0494	.0111	.0020	.0003	.0000					
1.0	.3679	.3679	.1839	.0613	.0153	.0031	.0005	.0001	.0000				
1.1	.3329	.3662	.2014	.0738	.0203	.0045	.0008	.0001	.0000				
1.2	.3012	.3614	.2169	.0867	.0260	.0062	.0012	.0001	.0000				
1.3	.2725	.3543	.2303	.0998	.0324	.0084	.0018	.0003	.0000	.0000			
1.4	.2466	.3452	.2417	.1128	.0395	.0111	.0026	.0005	.0001	.0000			
1.5	.2231	.3347	.2510	.1255	.0471	.0141	.0035	.0008	.0001	.0000			

1.6	.2019	.3230	.2584	.1378	.0551	.0176	.0047	.0011	.0002	.0000			
1.7	.1827	.3106	.2640	.1496	.0636	.0216	.0061	.0015	.0003	.0001	.0000		
1.8	.1653	.2975	.2678	.1607	.0723	.0260	.0078	.0020	.0005	.0001	.0000	.0000	.0000
1.9	.1496	.2842	.2700	.1710	.0812	.0309	.0098	.0027	.0006	.0001	.0000	.0000	.0000
2.0	.1353	.2707	.2707	.1804	.0902	.0361	.0120	.0034	.0009	.0002	.0000	.0000	.0000
2.2	.1108	.2438	.2681	.1966	.1082	.0476	.0174	.0055	.0015	.0004	.0001	.0000	.0000
2.4	.0907	.2177	.2613	.2090	.1254	.0602	.0241	.0083	.0025	.0007	.0002	.0000	.0000
2.6	.0743	.1931	.2510	.2176	.1414	.0735	.0319	.0118	.0038	.0011	.0003	.0001	.0000
2.8	.0608	.1703	.2384	.2225	.1557	.0872	.0407	.0163	.0057	.0018	.0005	.0001	.0000
3.0	.0498	.1494	.2240	.2240	.1680	.1008	.0504	.0216	.0081	.0027	.0008	.0002	.0001
3.2	.0408	.1304	.2087	.2226	.1781	.1140	.0608	.0278	.0111	.0040	.0013	.0004	.0001
3.4	.0334	.1135	.1929	.2186	.1858	.1264	.0716	.0348	.0148	.0056	.0019	.0006	.0002
3.6	.0273	.0984	.1771	.2125	.1912	.1377	.0826	.0425	.0191	.0076	.0028	.0009	.0003
3.8	.0224	.0850	.1617	.2046	.1944	.1477	.0936	.0508	.0241	.0102	.0039	.0013	.0004
4.0	.0183	.0733	.1465	.1954	.1954	.1563	.1042	.0595	.0298	.0132	.0053	.0019	.0006
5.0	.0067	.0337	.0842	.1404	.1755	.1755	.1462	.1044	.0653	.0363	.0181	.0082	.0034
6.0	.0025	.0149	.0446	.0892	.1339	.1606	.1606	.1377	.1033	.0688	.0413	.0225	.0113
7.0	.0009	.0064	.0223	.0521	.0912	.1277	.1490	.1490	.1304	.1014	.0710	.0452	.0264
8.0	.0003	.0027	.0107	.0286	.0573	.0916	.1221	.1396	.1396	.1241	.0993	.0722	.0481
9.0	.0001	.0011	.0050	.0150	.0337	.0607	.0911	.1171	.1318	.1318	.1186	.0970	.0728
10.0	.0000	.0005	.0023	.0076	.0189	.0378	.0631	.0901	.1126	.1251	.1251	.1137	.0948

(minutes). In our example, the mean inter-arrival time is $1/0.4 =$ 2.5 minutes. From this function one may calculate by integration the probability of, say, more than five minutes elapsing between the arrival of successive customers or the probability of two customers arriving within ten seconds of each other, etc.

Are these distributions likely to characterise the arrival behaviour of the customers in the grocery shop? There are reasons to believe that arrivals would not be completely at random: there are likely to be more customers at lunchtime or coffee break, and fewer customers when it rains, and people may come shopping with their friends, and so on. Nevertheless, it is remarkable that, in practice, these two theoretical probability distributions of arrivals (which are, in fact, two aspects of one distribution) *do* provide very good approximations to actual behaviour.

It also happens that exactly the same probability distributions can be used to characterise the service mechanism. In other words, it is often reasonable to describe the service time by a negative exponential distribution with mean $1/\mu$ (minutes) where $1/\mu$ is the average time to serve a customer (in minutes). Equivalently, one might describe the number of customers capable of being served (in one minute) by a Poisson distribution with mean μ. In our example, average service time is $1/\mu = 2$ minutes so the average number of customers capable of being served in a minute is $\mu = 0.5$.

An additional property of the negative exponential distribution is that the probability of a customer arriving at any time is independent of the time already elapsed since the previous arrival. Similarly, a service which has already taken three minutes is no more likely to be completed in the next five seconds than one which has taken only one minute.

The symbols λ and μ are used throughout queueing theory, as is the symbol ρ, meaning **traffic intensity**, defined by

$$\rho = \frac{\lambda}{\mu} = \frac{\text{average arrival rate}}{\text{average service rate}}$$

Here $\rho = 0.4/0.5 = 0.8$. One important condition of the model we shall describe is that the traffic intensity ρ be less than one; equivalently, the average arrival rate should be less than the average service rate (as in the present example). If this were not the case, queues of ever-increasing length would build up.

4   Results

The queues in a shop one minute after it opened would not present a fair picture of the day's operations because there would be insufficient time for any queue to build up. The following results describe the performance of a system once it has settled down into so-called **steady-state**. (It is not entirely clear how long this takes in practice: one theoretical study has suggested that half a day would be necessary.)

Recall that the situation consists of a single server and a single queue with first-in first-out queue discipline and Poisson or negative exponential arrival and service distributions with average arrival rate λ and average service rate μ (per unit time).

The probability of n customers in the system (i.e. being served or in the queue) is denoted P_n. In the present situation, this is given by

$$P_n = \left(1 - \frac{\lambda}{\mu}\right)\left(\frac{\lambda}{\mu}\right)^n = (1 - \rho)\rho^n \quad \text{for} \quad n = 0,1,2,\ldots \quad (1)$$

Since there is only one server, one person at most is being served at any time; any other customers in the system must be in the queue. As might be expected, the probabilities of all possible states of the system sum to unity ($\sum_{n=0}^{\infty} P_n = 1$), since $\sum_{n=0}^{\infty} \rho^n = 1/(1 - \rho)$ for $\rho < 1$. It is easily shown by induction that the probability of N or more customers in the system is

$$\sum_{n=N}^{\infty} P_n = \left(\frac{\lambda}{\mu}\right)^N = \rho^N \tag{2}$$

A customer has to wait for service whenever a queue exists, which is whenever there are one or more customers already in the system. The probability of this is one minus the probability of there being no one in the system, hence

$$\text{probability of a queue} = 1 - P_0 = \frac{\lambda}{\mu} = \rho \tag{3}$$

The following results are quite easily obtained.
Average number of customers in the system:

$$\frac{\lambda}{\mu - \lambda} \quad \text{or} \quad \frac{\rho}{1 - \rho} \tag{4}$$

Average number of customers in the queue:

$$\frac{\lambda^2}{\mu(\mu - \lambda)} \quad \text{or} \quad \frac{\rho^2}{1 - \rho} \tag{5}$$

Average time a customer spends in the system:

$$\frac{1}{\mu - \lambda} \quad \text{or} \quad \frac{1}{1 - \rho} \times \frac{1}{\mu} \tag{6}$$

Average time a customer spends in the queue:

$$\frac{\lambda}{\mu(\mu - \lambda)} \quad \text{or} \quad \frac{\rho}{1 - \rho} \times \frac{1}{\mu} \tag{7}$$

The last two expressions are in the same units of time as the
arrival and service rates. Various other results are also available
for this system.

We may now answer the questions posed at the beginning of
section 3 for the shop with $\lambda = 0.4$ and $\mu = 0.5$. The probability
of a customer having to wait for service (i.e. having to queue) is
$\rho = 0.8$, so that queues will be observed about 80% of the time.
The average number of customers in the queue will be $0.8^2 /$
$(1 - 0.8) = 3.2$. The average time spent waiting in the queue
will be $0.4/0.5(0.5 - 0.4) = 8$ minutes. This is a surprisingly 'bad'
performance for a shop which originally appeared to have more
than enough capacity to deal with its customers. But notice
how the average time a customer spends in the system depends
crucially on the traffic intensity, and increases rapidly as ρ tends
to one.

It is instructive to plot how the various aspects of performance depend upon λ and μ. Figure 1 illustrates for the average
time a customer spends in the system as given by equation (6).

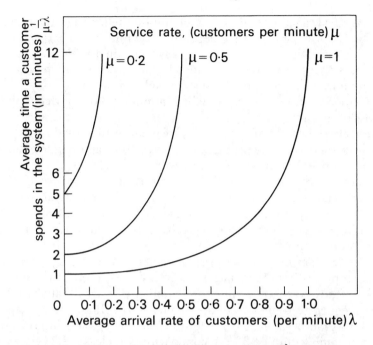

Figure 1. Relationship between arrival rate (λ), service rate (μ) and average time in system ($1/(\mu - \lambda)$)

5   Sensitivity analysis and optimisation

Queueing theory formulae are useful in exploring how system behaviour is likely to respond to changes in the parameters. In our simple example, one might ask: how fast must the single assistant work in order to reduce below 0.5 the probability of a customer having to wait for service? The probability in question is given by λ/μ, where $\lambda = 0.4$. In order that $0.4/\mu$ be less than 0.5 the service rate must exceed $0.4/0.5 = 0.8$ customers per minute, or 48 per hour (an average service time of $1/0.8 = 1.25$ minutes). Alternatively, if the assistant doubles his speed to $\mu = 1$ customer per minute we might ask how high an arrival rate could be handled before average time in the system exceeds six minutes. From figure 1 the answer may be read off as $\lambda = 0.83$ customers per minute.

In this way, the models may be used to help design the system, showing how performance depends upon number of servers, queue discipline, etc. The manager is concerned to design the 'best' system: this may mean the cheapest system which will function adequately, or the system yielding the least delay for a specified cost, or the system which minimises cost of delay plus cost of providing service. Typically, as the quality of service improves, the cost of delay falls but the cost of providing the service increases: the problem is to strike the right balance. Some simple optimisation models are described by Hillier.[5]

In practice, just as it is difficult to measure the cost of stock-outs (Chapters 11 and 12) so it is often difficult to measure the costs of delay. In the case of the grocery shop, the manager may not be worried about shoppers waiting except in so far as it causes them not to return, in which case the lost profit on sales is the relevant cost. Sometimes the delay is incurred by person-nel employed by the manager himself. For example, a classic early study was to determine the number of clerks that should be assigned to tool crib counters in use throughout the Boeing Aircraft factory area.[2] It was found that average waiting time of a mechanic would be 33.8 seconds with two clerks, 4.7 seconds with three clerks and 0.8 seconds with four clerks. On average there were 540 mechanics calling at the tool crib per day. Suppose that a clerk costs $3 per hour for a 7½ hour day and that a mechanic's time is worth $7 per hour. If the number of clerks is increased from two to three then the value of the saving in mechanics' idle time is

$$\frac{540 \times (33.8 - 4.7)}{60 \times 60} \times \$7 = \$30.56 \text{ per day}$$

while the cost of employing the extra clerk is:

7½ x $3 = $22.50 per day

Employing the third clerk would yield a net saving of $8.06 per day. It may be verified that the saving in mechanics' idle time from employing a fourth clerk would be outweighed by the cost of doing so.

Another general problem involves the balancing of the cost of operatives against the lost profit from machine down-time (see exercise 6). This is known as the **machine interference** problem. The manager has to decide how many operatives to employ and whether to organise the machines into separate groups with their own operatives or to let all machines be tended by all operatives. This is a familiar problem in the textile industry; Courtaulds regularly uses queueing theory here.

Page[8] describes the following problem which arose in a study by H. Ashcroft.[1] Contrary to first impressions, it is formally the same as the machine interference problem.

> Ingots of steel are heated to the temperature required for rolling in soaking pits. The time taken to heat the ingots is very variable and can be assumed to have a negative exponential distribution. There is one rolling mill which reduces the ingots to slabs. The time taken to roll the ingots from a soaking pit is constant. On continuous working sufficient pits must be provided to ensure that the mill is not delayed by more than one hour a week on average because there are no ingots ready to roll in the soaking pits. The average time to heat a pit of ingots to be ready for rolling is 3 hours. The time taken to roll the ingots in a pit is 20 minutes. What is the smallest number of soaking pits needed to provide the specified utilisation of the mill?
>
> Treating the mill as the operative, and the pits as machines, the problem becomes a machine interference problem with constant repair time of 20 minutes (the rolling time for a pit) and exponential running time (the heating time). A single operative (the mill) looks after the machines, and the requirement is that the operative must be busy for not less than $167/168 = 99.40\%$ of the time. Results for this model are tabulated in Ashcroft[1] and the number of soaking pits required is calculated as 15.

6   Extensions of the simple queueing model

The model described so far has involved negative exponential (or Poisson) arrival and service distributions and a single server.

Table 2 Average waiting time of customers in a simple Poisson queueing system (expressed in units of average service time)

Utilisation ρ/n	Number of servers (n)								
	2	3	4	5	6	7	8	9	10
0.1	0.0101	0.0014	0.0002	0.0000	0.0000	0.0000	0.0000	0.0000	0.0000
0.2	0.0417	0.0103	0.0030	0.0010	0.0003	0.0001	0.0000	0.0000	0.0000
0.3	0.0989	0.0333	0.0132	0.0058	0.0027	0.0013	0.0006	0.0003	0.0002
0.4	0.1905	0.0784	0.0378	0.0199	0.0111	0.0064	0.0039	0.0024	0.0015
0.5	0.3333	0.1579	0.0870	0.0521	0.0330	0.0218	0.0148	0.0102	0.0072
0.6	0.5625	0.2956	0.1794	0.1181	0.0819	0.0589	0.0436	0.0330	0.0253
0.7	0.9608	0.5470	0.3572	0.2519	0.1867	0.1432	0.1128	0.0906	0.0739
0.8	1.7778	1.0787	0.7455	0.5541	0.4315	0.3471	0.2860	0.2401	0.2046
0.9	4.2632	2.7235	1.9693	1.5250	1.2335	1.0285	0.8769	0.7606	0.6687

Similar formulae may be deduced for the same model with multiple servers. It is often easier to present these formulae in the form of tables. Table 2 shows how average waiting time is related to number of servers (n) and traffic intensity (ρ). Consider the previous grocery shop example where average service time is $1/\mu = 2$ minutes and traffic intensity is $\rho = 0.8$. If there were now $n = 2$ servers then utilisation would be $\rho/n = 0.4$. Average time spent waiting in the queue would be 0.1905 times 2 minutes = 0.38 minutes, a substantial reduction from 10 minutes.

Formulae are available for a variety of other arrival and service distributions, and for various queue disciplines, e.g. situations involving balking, and where the servers give priority to different classes of customers (as at many computer installations). Recently, work has begun on the problem of designing an optimal price schedule for different grades of service provided.

One of the most common situations involves a maximum limit on the queue size. This is typically the case on telephone switchboards, where only a limited number of calls can be held. The next chapter describes such a situation at West Midlands Gas and the model used to analyse it; exercise 6 at the end of this chapter gives some of the relevant formulae.

References and further reading

1   Ashcroft H., 'The productivity of several machines under the care of one operator', *Journal of the Royal Statistical Society*, Series B, vol. 12, no. 1, 1950.

2   Brigham G., 'On a congestion problem in an aircraft factory', *Operations Research*, vol. 3, no. 4, 1955.

3   Edie L. C., 'Traffic delays at toll booths', *Operations Research*, vol. 2, no. 2, 1954.

4   Friend J. K., 'Two studies in airport congestion', *Operational Research Quarterly*, vol. 9, no. 3, 1958.

5   Hillier F. S., 'Cost models for the application of priority waiting line theory to industrial problems', *Journal of Industrial Engineering*, vol. 16, no. 3, 1965.

6   Lee A., *Applied Queueing Theory*, Macmillan 1966.

7   Morse P. M., *Queues, Inventories and Maintenance*, Wiley 1958.

8   Page E., *Queueing Theory in OR*, Butterworths 1972.

9   Syski R., *Introduction to Congestion Theory in Telephone Systems*, Oliver and Boyd 1960.

10   Tocher K. D., 'The role of models in operational research', *Journal of the Royal Statistical Society*, Part 2, 1961.

Exercises

1   If customers arrive according to a Poisson distribution with mean of 2 per minute, what are the probabilities that in any one minute the number of arrivals is (a) 0, (b) 3, (c) between 1 and 3 inclusive, (d) 4 or over?

2   In the simple example of the grocer's shop discussed in the text, calculate the performance of the system if a different assistant is hired instead of the present one, where the new assistant can work at twice the rate of the previous one.

3   In the same simple example, with the original assistant, how far would customer arrival rate have to fall before average waiting time reduced to three minutes?

4   A telephone switchboard receives an average of 40 calls per hour and each call lasts two minutes on average. If it is required that there should be a line free at least 90% of the time, how many lines need to be installed? (Assume inter-arrival times and holding times are distributed exponentially.) *Hint:* Use formula from equation 6 for $q = 0$.

5   A set of machines breaks down in a Poisson fashion at an average rate of two per hour. Machine idle time is assumed to cost £5 per hour in value of lost output. The repairman can service machines in an average time of 15 minutes (from the time he starts on the machine) where repair time is distributed exponentially. A new testing gauge is available which will cost £1,000 but will cut average repair time to 10 minutes. Should the gauge be purchased? (Assume an 8 hour day, 5 day week, 50 week year.)

6   For the system described in the next chapter, where there is a limited queue length q, Syski[9] has shown that the steady state probabilities are given by

$$P_n = \begin{cases} \dfrac{\rho^n}{n!} P_0 & 0 \leqslant n \leqslant c \\[3mm] \dfrac{\rho^n}{c!c^{n-c}} P_0 & c \leqslant n \leqslant c + q \end{cases}$$

P_0, the probability of the system being empty, is obtained by solving for

$$\sum_{n=0}^{c+q} P_n = 1$$

hence

$$1/P_0 = \sum_{n=0}^{c-1} \frac{\rho^n}{n!} + \sum_{n=c}^{c+q} \frac{\rho^n}{c!c^{n-c}}$$

Calculate the probabilities of there being 0, 1, 2 and 3 customers in the system when there are 2 servers and a maximum queue length of 1. Assume $\lambda = 0.8$, $\mu = 1.0$.

14

Manning the Telephone Enquiry Bureau at West Midlands Gas*

L B SPARROW

1   Introduction

All telephone enquiries to West Midlands Gas are dealt with by a team of specialist clerks in two centralised enquiry bureaux. Customers anywhere in the Region can contact a bureau at local call costs. At all times it is essential to maintain a high standard of answering service, not only because this is expected by the customer for any type of enquiry but also to ensure that emergency calls relating, perhaps, to gas leaks are accepted and dealt with.

In about 1970 the enquiry bureaux were finding it difficult to maintain the servicing of customers' calls at peak periods with the existing monitoring equipment. It was decided to set up a queueing theory model of the telephone answering system. The aim was to derive the relationships between traffic level, grade of service, waiting time and manning levels within the bureaux. The model would be used as a planning tool, both for indicating peak manning requirements and for optimising number of staff at off-peak times. This chapter describes the model which was developed and the results which were obtained.

---

*This paper describes the work of Mrs P. Bishop who was a member of the Corporate Planning Department at West Midlands Gas from 1964 to 1971.

2 Description of the system

The automatic call distribution system (ACD) installed at West Midlands Gas headquarters operates as follows. Incoming calls pass through the automatic call queueing device in strict order of arrival and are allocated in cyclic order to those service positions which are manned. If there are no free positions, the caller waits in the queue, where he hears a ringing tone until he is answered by the next available operator. If the calls in the system equal the combined capacity of the operators and the queue, the incoming call is rejected and the caller receives an 'engaged' tone. The maximum queue length can be set to suit the operating conditions.

3 Application of queueing theory

The situation is quite evidently a queueing system with many servers and a limited queue length. The ACD system ensures a single queue with a strict first-come, first-served queue discipline and full availability of operators to all calls, i.e. calls cannot be rejected or queued while any operator is available to answer the call.

It was assumed that calls arrived at random from an infinite number of sources, so that the inter-arrival times had a negative exponential distribution and the number of calls within a given time interval had a Poisson distribution. This was a reasonable assumption, since there was a large number of customers acting independently of each other, as long as the grade of service achieved was good enough to ensure few repeated calls.

The service time was assumed to be negatively exponentially distributed, i.e. the probability of a call finishing at any time is independent of the duration of the call up to that time. Figure 1 illustrates the nature of this assumption. The histogram was drawn from data on call durations taken at an off-peak time. The exponential fit is a good one. At peak times the exponential fit is not so good, but there is still a long tail to the distribution and the average call duration is not significantly different. Call duration here includes any paperwork which might be necessary

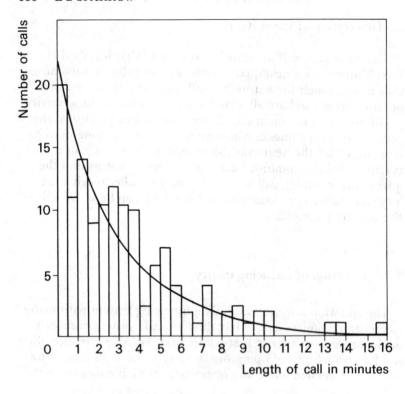

Figure 1. Histogram showing number of calls of a given length at half-minute intervals. The curve shows the expected number of calls of a given length from a negative exponential distribution with mean call length 3·322 minutes

immediately after the call, since the operator is not available to the ADC system while this paperwork is being carried out.

Using the notation introduced in the previous chapter, let λ denote the average calling rate, measured in number of calls arriving per minute; let μ denote the average serving rate, measured in number of calls dealt with per minute ($1/\mu$ is the average call duration measured in minutes); let $\rho = \lambda/\mu$ denote the traffic intensity, that is, the average number of calls arriving in the average service time; let P_n denote the steady-state probability that there are n calls in the system, either being dealt with or waiting in the queue; let c denote the number of telephone operators and let q denote the maximum capacity of the queue of calls being held.

The steady-state probabilities P_n for this system may be expressed in terms of the parameters ρ, c and q (see exercise 6 in Chapter 13).

There are two important criteria in the management of a telephone system: grade of service and waiting time. The next task is to obtain expressions for these in terms of the system parameters λ, μ, c and q.

4   Grade of service

Grade of service, denoted by g, is defined as the proportion of calls which are lost, i.e. the ratio of lost calls to calls offered. Lost calls are those which receive the engaged tone.

It may be shown that grade of service is numerically equal to the probability P_{c+q} that the system is completely full. Hence (from exercise 6 of Chapter 13) g is related to the parameters λ, μ, c and q by the function

$$g = \frac{\rho^{c+q}}{c!c^q} P_0$$

To appreciate this relationship, it is necessary to represent it graphically. Figure 2 shows how grade of service is related to number of operators and to maximum queue setting for specified average arrival rate $\lambda = 15$ calls per minute and average call duration $1/\mu = 3.322$ minutes. Thus a grade of service of one call lost in 10 can be obtained with 46 operators and maximum queue setting of 10 calls, or with 50 operators and a maximum queue setting of zero, or with various combinations in between. Note that the equal grade of service contours are practically vertical. This implies that changing the queue setting has a negligible effect on grade of service compared with the effect of changing the number of operators.

The grade of service predicted by the model was compared with actual values measured on the ACD system, and a good correspondence was found.

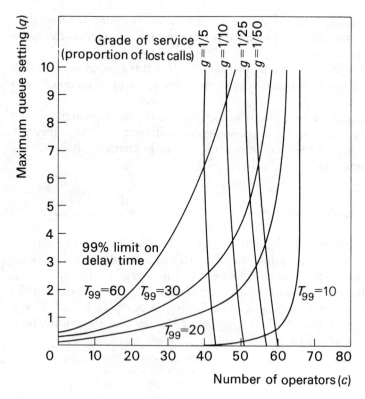

Figure 2. Graph showing contours of constant g and T_{99} for $\lambda = 15, 1/\mu = 3\cdot322$

5   Waiting time

Waiting time, T, is the length of time that a caller is kept waiting in the queue before he is allocated to an operator. It is not possible to obtain T as an explicit mathematical function of the various system parameters. However, it is possible to obtain an indirect expression for the probability that the waiting time of accepted calls will exceed any specified time t. Let T_{99} denote that waiting time which is not exceeded in 99% of the accepted calls (hence is suffered by only 1% of the accepted calls).

Using Newton's method of iteration, a computer programme was written to calculate values of T_{99} as a function of the parameters λ, μ, c and q. Figure 2 plots the contours of constant T_{99} (in seconds) against number of operators and queue setting for the previously specified values $\lambda = 15$ calls per minute and $1/\mu = 3.322$ minutes. Thus, the contour for $T_{99} = 30$ shows that 99% of the calls accepted will wait less than 30 seconds if there are about 57 operators with a queue setting of 10 calls, or about 50 operators and a queue setting of four calls, or about 20 operators and a queue setting of one call. The slopes of these curves show that when a low waiting time is specified (say, less than 10 seconds), the required number of operators is quite rigid (somewhat over 60) and the queue setting has negligible effect. When a long waiting time is allowed (say, one minute) there is a fairly constant trade-off between queue setting and operators, with five operators compensating for an increase of one call in the queue setting.

6 Use of the model

It is apparent from figure 2 that, for a given queue setting, increasing the number of operators improves both the grade of service and the waiting time. However, for a given number of operators, an increase in the queue setting improves the grade of service but worsens the waiting time (because more calls are accepted but they have to wait longer to be answered).

It was decided that the grade of service should be maintained at one lost call in 25 and that 99% of the accepted calls should not have to wait longer than 20 seconds. The intersection of the $g = 1/25$ contour and the $T_{99} = 20$ contour in figure 2 shows that, for the specified traffic conditions λ and μ, a maximum queue setting of four calls is required with at least 55 telephone operators.

The model was originally designed to indicate staff requirements at various times of the day. Using a computer, it was possible to plot out in figure 3 the queue settings and operator requirements against the average call rate λ for any chosen performance criteria, and for specified average holding times $1/\mu$. Figure 3 shows such a planning graph for the criteria $g = 1/25$

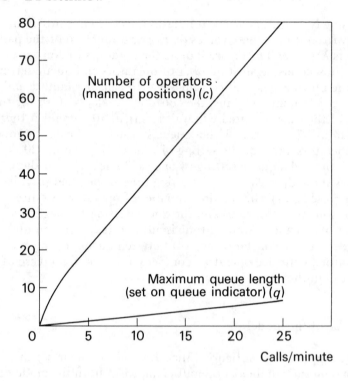

Figure 3. Planning graph, showing values of c and q for different call rates such as to give $g=1$ lost call in 25 and $T_{99}=20$ seconds

and $T_{99} = 20$ seconds, with $1/\mu = 3.322$ minutes as before. Thus, if call rates fell to 5 calls per minute during slack periods the queue setting should be reduced to 1 or 2 and less than 20 operators would be required. For an average call rate of 20 per minute about 70 operators would be required.

7   Reservations

Certain reservations on the use of the model must be borne in mind.

1   The graph shows the number of positions manned, not the staffing of the ACD system. Work study measurements must be used to make allowances for rest periods, etc. to give a ratio between operators available and positions manned.

2   Some calls require the operator to hold and enquire from another department. Any increase in manning should be matched on these other departments so that no extra delays are caused, otherwise the mean call length will increase. Under such circumstances, figure 3 would no longer be valid.

3   At peak times it may be impracticable to man to the required grade of service. Other methods of improving service can then be brought into use. One method is to reduce the call length. This can be done by leaving busy hour paperwork to be dealt with later, or by speeding up certain types of call. For example, account queries could be answered immediately if the telephone operator could access the customer's computer record via a visual display console.

4   At peak times all lines from Solihull telephone exchange to the ACD system may be in use while some operators are waiting for a call. Under these circumstances, the first assumption made in section 3 is not valid, and calls are being lost even though the queue is not full. If the number of lines from the exchange were increased until congestion no longer took place, the queueing model would again become valid and figure 3 could be used to determine peak manning requirements.

8   Further developments

We have described the initial study of the ACD system as it existed in 1971. Since that time telephone traffic has increased considerably and this has entailed extensions to the system. A two-stage ACD is now in operation which allows the maintenance of answering standards throughout the day and throughout the year with varying traffic levels while ensuring the efficient use of manpower. The chapter has attempted to show how queueing theory has played a useful part in the successful development of this system.

15

Computer Simulation Methods

M PIDD

1 Introduction

The previous chapters of this book have been mainly concerned with analytical techniques which can be used to solve business problems. These OR techniques have enjoyed widespread success in many situations, but there are many problems which are just not amenable to solution by their use. To use such techniques we must decide which variables are relevant and develop some relationships between them so as to form a mathematical model of the situation. But many business situations are so fuzzy that we cannot with certainty state which variables are important. Moreover, the relationships between them may be too complex to solve mathematically. For such problems, computer simulation methods offer a very powerful approach to developing a solution.

A simulation approach can be useful for determining and developing control mechanisms for existing systems. For example, such work has been undertaken by the University of Leeds Bus Operations Research Unit on the subject of the control of bus operations. They have been attempting to answer questions like:

What is the effect of linking buses to a central radio control?
What is the effect of introducing dial and ride services?

These could, of course, be assessed by practical experimentation, but it is much cheaper and more flexible to use a simulation approach.

Simulation is also a useful way of getting to grips with very complex situations. We may not understand how a real system actually operates, and hence all we can do is embody our beliefs about the real system in a model. We use a simulation approach to manipulate the model and we change the structure of the model until its behaviour corresponds with that of the real world.

An example of a simulation study with this aim is the work done by Meadows et al. for the Club of Rome in attempting to assess the prospects for the year 2000 for the entire world. Whether or not one agrees with their prognostications, this study is certainly an attempt to explore the complex structure of a real system.

Finally, we may wish to design a completely new system. For example, we might wish to ascertain the facilities needed in a large building to cope with the inevitable breakdown of equipment and to minimise its effect. The next chapter describes how a large British motor manufacturer used a simulation approach to cope with this very problem.

In so far as many OR techniques involve advanced mathematics with which the average manager is not familiar, he may find it difficult to understand what the OR man is doing. To conduct a simulation study, a rather different sort of ability is required, one which the manager possesses — the ability to recognise the structure of a situation. For this reason, a simulation approach can make for much greater teamwork between the manager and the OR scientist.

On the other hand, simulation has its drawbacks. Large amounts of data are often required, and these need careful compilation, collation and analysis. Computer programmes must be designed, programmed, tested and run. All these activities can turn out to be very expensive.

Moreover, there is no guarantee that the results will be conclusive. Because of the emphasis on the overall structure of the situation, rather than on the details, the results may not be too accurate.

Finally, a simulation model will not of itself suggest policies or improvements; all it can do is to evaluate possibilities put forward by managers or OR men.

Thus, the decision to use simulation requires careful consideration.

2   The nature of simulation

A useful and concise definition of simulation is given by
Ackoff and Sasieni.[1]

> Models REPRESENT reality, simulation IMITATES it. Simu-
> lation always involves the manipulation of a model; it is, in
> effect, a way of manipulating a model so that it yields a
> motion picture of reality.

In this chapter, we are concerned with the ways in which we
can use a model to imitate reality. Ideally, we should like to
manipulate a model so that its behaviour is identical with that of
the real situation. Clearly, this will never be possible, but that
is our goal.

One of the problems about the use of mathematical models
in OR is that they tend to be static and concerned with the
'steady state'. When the system being represented by such
models undergoes major or even minor upheavals, the models
tend not to be adequate for representing the dynamics of the
situation. However, simulation is aimed at copying the dynamics
of the real situation and at predicting actual behaviour.

Most of the OR techniques described in this book are mathematical models of varying degrees of complexity. Simulation
methods, however, usually make use of **logical models** as the
basis of their attempts to copy the dynamics of a real situation.
Such logical models do not usually use mathematics directly;
they are best represented in the form of a flow-chart which
shows how, and in what sequence, the factors relevant to a
situation interact. Later on in this chapter, activity cycle diagrams will be introduced as one such method of charting the
logic of a system. It is, of course, possible to use the more
general type of flow charts as employed by computer systems
personnel and industrial engineers.

The next step is to transfer the logical models on to a computer. Computer programming is necessary in most realistic
simulations simply because of the length of time taken to carry

out a simulation manually. The speed and memory of modern computers have taken much of the work out of simulation studies. The computer may be accessed by using general purpose languages (such as FORTRAN or ALGOL) or special languages. These special languages are designed for simulation applications only and carry features common to all simulation studies. The more recent languages are very similar to spoken English and some are designed to allow the user to write the programme conversationally with the computer.

The construction of a suitable model is essential to any simulation study, but it is generally agreed that this is not the most important phase in such a project. The essential feature in simulation is the way in which the model is put to work in an attempt to copy the dynamic operation of the real system. The analyst, therefore, must concentrate on getting as much information as possible from as little computer time as possible. Doing this requires the use of methods to reduce the variance of the results, finding ways of running the model efficiently and finding easier ways of communicating with the computer. These are the principal areas of research in computer simulation for use in OR.

3   Types of simulation

There are four major ways of simulating management problems; not all approaches are similar for any given situation.

1   **Stochastic digital simulation** — This is often called the Monte Carlo method because early applications used roulette wheels to simulate the chance events inherent in its approach. Programmes are usually written for a digital computer (the type used by most firms for their general data processing) which is used principally for its speed and data handling capacity. The Monte Carlo technique is the major preoccupation of this chapter.

2   **System dynamics** — In effect, this method uses a digital computer to simulate an analogue computer which is simulating

the real situation! This technique will be discussed in the last section of this chapter.

3   **Financial and corporate modelling** — Now that computer technology makes it possible for a large number of users simultaneously to use a computer via remote terminals, this particular approach shows increasing popularity. Computer programmes are written which represent the financial structure of the business and the computer technology allows the user to converse effectively with the model. Hence various policies may be examined and the most suitable selected.

4   **Operational gaming** — This is typified by the competitive business games in which teams manage hypothetical organisations in competition for a market; these games are widely used in training. The aim is to set up an accurate model of the situation and allow people to operate it so as to learn about the real world without the expense of real mistakes. Games are often used in studying conflict, e.g. war games.

Corporate models and business games are unfortunately beyond the scope of this book.

The remainder of the chapter outlines some of the important concepts of simulation methods. We begin by discussing the formulation of a simulation model in terms of activity cycle diagrams. This is followed by a numerical example illustrating the use of the Monte Carlo sampling method. The chapter concludes with a brief outline of the system dynamics approach.

4   Model formulation: activity cycle diagrams

A logical model is complete when all the relevant components of the system are known, when the variables and parameters making up the components are identified and when the relationships between the components, variables and parameters are specified. Such formulation is rather more of an art than a science and requires experience in the use of certain tools.

In specifying the relevant components and their constituent variables, the 'principle of parsimony' should be borne in mind. (This has been alternatively described elsewhere as **KISS**: Keep

TOTAL SYSTEM

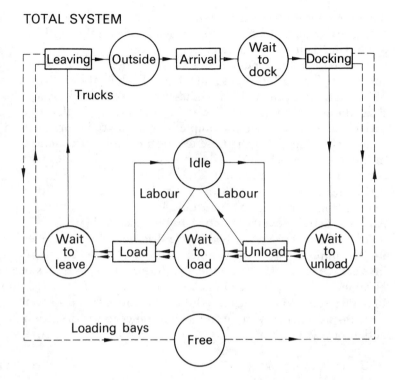

Figure 1. Activity cycle diagram for warehouse example

it Simple, Stupid.) Its obvious message is that instead of going overboard with as complicated a view of the problem as possible and later chopping away the dead wood, we should begin with a simple model and refine it as necessary. Indeed, as emphasised in Chapter 2, an important aspect of OR modelling in general and of simulation in particular, is the backtracking which occurs as more understanding of the problem is gained.

We need to begin with the functional components of the system and specify their interrelationships in a simple manner. One way of doing this, although not the only one, is by careful use of **activity cycle diagrams**. Consider the following example. A warehouse includes a loading platform with five loading bays at which loaded trucks arrive at irregular intervals; the trucks must queue if no bay is free. On docking into the bay, the trucks are unloaded when labour is available and then re-loaded, again when labour is available.

The major components of this system, called the **entities**, are the loading bays, the trucks and labour. Each of these entities has an activity cycle which includes **live states** (activities) and **dead states** (waiting). Both live and dead states generally take a variable amount of time to complete, with the time for the dead states depending upon the time taken to complete the activities in the live states. Thus, the labour activity cycle includes the activities of loading and unloading and the dead state of being idle (waiting for lorries to arrive). The loading bays are either occupied or free, whereas the trucks have a more complex cycle. All three activity cycles may be combined as in figure 1.

The principal use of activity cycle diagrams is to obtain an understanding of how the various components of the system interact. Once a sufficient understanding of the system has been obtained, one may proceed to simulation itself. The next section illustrates the Monte Carlo method of sampling in a problem which is sufficiently simple to make it unnecessary first to draw activity cycle diagrams.

5   Example of the Monte Carlo method

Aslan Manufacturing Ltd operates a bank of power presses which stamp out shallow metal containers. One of their presses, the Narnia Mark II, has two identical dies, A and B, which must be periodically replaced. The replacement dies cost £40 each and the act of replacement (i.e. dismantling, reassembly and lost production) costs £100. This latter cost is the same whether one or both dies are replaced. Consequently, it may be cheaper to replace both dies when one fails than to replace only the die which fails. Aslan Manufacturing wish to determine which of these two replacement policies will minimise their total costs.

The works engineer has collected historical data on the life of the dies, as shown in the first two columns of table 1. Thus, there is a 10% chance that a die will fail in its first week, a 15% chance that it will fail in its second week, and so on. The

Table 1   Life expectancy for Narnia Mark II dies

Life (weeks)	Probability	Associated range of random numbers
1	0.10	00 — 09
2	0.15	10 — 24
3	0.20	25 — 44
4	0.35	45 — 79
5	0.15	80 — 94
6	0.05	95 — 99
	1.00	

maximum life of a die is six weeks. For simplicity, it will be assumed that the die fails only at the end of a week.

In the present case, it is comparatively simple to compare the two policies using methods of classical statistics: the interested reader may care to attempt this. However, we shall use the situation to show how the Monte Carlo method may be employed.

The basic idea is to generate a series of lives for the two dies, which is consistent with the previous known data, and to see which of the two alternative policies performs best in this hypothetical situation. The Monte Carlo method involves taking a series of random numbers, one for each die, and associating with each random number a life (in weeks) for that die. In order that the resulting life distribution be consistent with previous experience, the number of random numbers associated with a particular life must be proportional to the probability of that life occurring, as given by table 1.

We shall use a table of random numbers, as given in table 2. These random numbers range between 00 and 99, and any number in that range has an equal probability of occurring in any position. The obvious way of associating these random numbers to the die lives is to let the first 10 numbers of the range (i.e. 00 to 09) be associated with a life of one week, the next 15 numbers (10 to 24) with a life of two weeks, and so on, as shown in the third column of table 1.

The next step is to write down a stream of random numbers and find the corresponding lines. For die A we shall start in the

Table 2   Random numbers

*29 94 98 94 24	34 67 35 48 76	80 95 90 90 17	75 24 63 38 24
64 49 69 10 82	24 80 52 40 37	20 63 61 04 02	64 05 18 81 59
53 75 91 93 30	23 20 90 25 60	15 95 33 47 64	26 89 80 93 54
34 25 20 57 27	38 31 13 11 65	88 67 67 43 97	45 42 72 68 42
40 48 73 51 92	64 03 23 66 53	98 95 11 68 77	01 39 09 22 86
+00 39 68 29 61	36 69 73 61 70	65 81 33 98 85	87 37 92 52 41
66 37 32 20 30	35 30 34 26 14	86 79 90 74 39	20 11 74 52 04
77 84 57 03 29	68 66 57 48 18	73 05 38 52 47	01 75 87 53 79
10 45 65 04 26	90 55 35 75 48	28 46 82 87 09	19 47 60 72 46
11 04 96 67 24	35 80 83 42 82	60 93 52 03 44	36 16 81 08 51
14 90 56 86 07	22 10 94 05 58	60 97 09 34 33	45 86 25 10 25
39 80 82 77 32	50 72 56 82 48	29 40 52 42 01	96 11 96 38 96
06 28 89 80 83	13 74 67 00 78	18 47 54 06 10	33 35 13 54 62
86 50 75 84 01	36 76 66 79 01	90 36 47 64 93	83 60 94 97 00
87 51 76 49 69	91 82 60 89 28	93 78 56 13 68	77 28 14 40 77
17 46 85 09 50	58 04 77 69 74	73 03 95 71 86	05 56 70 70 07
17 72 70 80 15	45 31 82 23 74	21 11 57 82 53	15 95 66 00 00
77 40 27 72 14	43 23 60 02 10	45 52 16 42 37	40 41 92 15 85
66 25 22 91 48	36 93 68 72 03	76 62 11 39 90	43 66 79 45 43
14 22 56 85 14	46 42 75 67 88	96 29 77 88 22	34 88 88 15 53
68 47 92 76 86	46 16 28 35 54	94 75 08 99 23	61 96 27 93 35
26 94 03 68 58	70 29 73 41 35	53 14 03 33 40	54 69 28 23 91
85 15 74 79 54	32 97 92 65 75	57 60 04 08 81	77 97 45 00 24
11 10 00 20 40	12 86 07 46 97	96 64 48 94 39	13 02 12 48 92
16 50 53 44 84	40 21 95 25 63	43 65 17 70 82	93 91 08 36 47
26 45 74 77 74	71 92 43 37 29	65 39 45 95 93	86 74 31 71 57
95 27 07 99 53	59 36 78 38 48	82 39 61 01 18	18 74 39 24 23
67 89 75 43 87	54 62 24 44 31	91 19 04 25 92	66 67 43 68 06
97 34 40 87 21	16 86 84 87 67	02 07 11 20 59	59 04 79 00 33
73 20 88 98 37	68 93 59 14 16	26 25 22 96 63	01 54 03 54 56

top left-hand corner of the table and work across the first block row by row. Thus, the first number 29 (indicated by*) lies in the range 25—44 and represents a life of three weeks. For die B we shall work similarly from the second block of numbers, beginning with 00 (indicated by +). The results are shown in table 3.

Table 3   Random sampling to determine die lives

Die no.	Die A		Die B	
	Random numbers	Life	Random numbers	Life
1	29*	3	00+	1
2	94	5	39	3
3	98	6	68	4
4	94	5	29	3
5	24	2	61	4
6	64	4	66	4
7	49	4	37	3
8	69	4	32	3
9	10	2	20	2
10	82	5	30	3
11	53	4	77	4
12	75	4	84	5
13	91	5	57	4
14	93	5	03	1
15	30	3	29	3
16	34	3	10	2
17	25	3	45	4

This table may be used to evaluate the two policies over a simulated time period of 50 weeks, as shown in table 4.

Separate replacement policy   Examination of table 4 shows that die A is replaced a total of 12 times in the 50 weeks. Die B is replaced a total of 16 times but four of these occur at the same times as replacements for die A. Hence, the total cost of this policy is:

Cost of dies   = £40 × (12 + 16)   = £1,120

Replacement cost = £100 × (12 + 16 − 4) = £2,400

Total cost   £3,520

Joint replacement policy   Table 4 also shows the joint cumulative time life of the two dies using the shorter of the two lives as

Table 4   Comparison of two replacement policies

Separate replacement policy				Joint replacement policy		
Die A no.	Cumulative life	Die B no.	Cumulative life	Dies no.	Minimum joint life	Cumulative joint life
1	3	1	1	1	1	1
2	8	2	4	2	3	4
3	14	3	8	3	4	8
4	19	4	11	4	3	11
5	21	5	15	5	2	13
6	25	6	19	6	4	17
7	29	7	22	7	3	20
8	33	8	25	8	3	23
9	35	9	27	9	2	25
10	40	10	30	10	3	38
11	44	11	34	11	4	32
12	48	12	39	12	4	36
(13)	(53)	13	43	13	4	40
		14	44	14	1	41
		15	47	15	3	44
		16	49	16	2	46
				17	3	49

the joint life. This shows that replacing both dies when one fails leads to a total of 17 joint replacements over the 50 weeks. Hence the total cost of this policy is:

Cost of dies   =   £40 x 34 = £1,360

Replacement cost = £100 x 17 = £1,700

Total cost   £3,060

6   Interpreting the results

It would seem at first sight that the results of the Narnia Mark II replacement problem are straightforward. They seem to indicate that joint replacement is cheaper than single replacement by £460 over a 50-week period. However, this does not necessarily mean that the difference in costs between the two policies will be exactly £460 in practice. If, instead of starting at the points indicated by * and + in the random number table, we had started elsewhere, this would mean that we would have drawn a different random sample from the life distribution of the dies. This would have produced results slightly different from those shown.

It is usual, therefore, to make several simulation runs each with a distinct random sampling pattern. Techniques are available[4] for deciding how many runs are required in a given situation. The golden rule in examining the results produced by a simulation is the one which underlies all classical statistics: caution allied to rational argument. No simulation study should be completed on the basis of a single finished computer run. If the results are that obvious and clear cut, the simulation was probably superfluous anyway.

We have now seen that the Monte Carlo method is a way of taking random samples from probability distributions. In our example, we had three such probability distributions: one for the life of each die and one for their joint life. We took samples from these to produce a synthetic history of the two replacement policies which were under consideration. When discussing the use of activitity cycle diagrams, we said that each live state had a probability distribution associated with it. The process of Monte Carlo simulation involves taking random samples from these distributions. The order and rate at which these samples are taken is determined by the dynamic logic of the activity cycle diagram. Hence we may simulate the dynamic behaviour of the system under investigation.

7   System dynamics

Alongside Monte Carlo simulation methods, a quite distinct form of computer simulation is enjoying increasing use. It has various titles, but the most common are **system dynamics** or **industrial dynamics**. This method is the product of work done by Forrester[2] and others at the Massachusetts Institute of Technology and has been applied in industry, commerce, government and in the global efforts of the Club of Rome.

The system dynamics approach is a development of the servo-mechanism control theory widely used in electrical engineering.

The underlying assumption is that socio-economic systems may be regarded as analogous to servomechanisms and central to this analogy is the idea of **feedback of information.**

A decision is made which leads to action, but there is a time-lag or delay between the decision to act and the act itself. The action leads to results, once again following a delay of some magnitude. The results are then fed back to the decision maker as information on which to base a further decision and so on. The situation is complicated yet further by the realisation that the information may well be distorted before it reaches the decision maker and that there will probably be delays in its transmission.

What these characteristics mean is that the system will have properties which are quite distinct from those found in the elements which compose it. This being the case, it is necessary to view the system as a whole and not just as a collection of parts. If we wish to improve the overall performance of a system, we must analyse the total system and not merely attempt to optimise the parts. Hence to undertake a stock control project in isolation from the capabilities of the factory and the charac-teristics of the customers would be short-sighted.

Applications of system dynamics in the UK have been largely confined to academic studies. OR in this country has tradition-ally been interested principally in 'one-off' decisions, whereas the system dynamic method is relevant to the design of interacting systems. It is generally regarded as a method of examining large systems at a level which allows little detail. As such, it is a speculative tool and few OR workers are adequately trained in its method; however, as the design of on-going systems becomes an increasing preoccupation, it is to be expected that its use may increase. It must be conceded that studies using it are unlikely to produce the direct cost savings that are often required of industrial OR and, as long as this situation continues, applica-tions will remain limited.

References and further reading

1   Ackoff R. L. and Sasieni M. W., *Fundamentals of Operations Research*, Wiley 1968.

2   Forrester J., *Industrial Dynamics*, MIT/Wiley 1961.

3   Meadows D. H., *The Limits to Growth*, Earth Island 1972.

4   Naylor T. L. *et al.*, *Computer Simulation Techniques*, Wiley 1966.

Exercises

1   Repeat the Narnia Mark II simulation starting at different points in the random number table. How many repetitions are required to give a reliable result?

2   A Post Office which currently experiences frequent queues when operating two counters is considering a third. You are asked to prepare a simulation study and illustrate its operation.

Two items of information are available, measured over 100 customers. Table 1 sets out a frequency distribution of customer inter-arrival times. Table 2 sets out a frequency distribution of

Table 1   Inter-arrival time of customers

Interval	Frequency
Less than 10 seconds	20
10—20 secs	40
20—30 secs	25
30—60 secs	7
60—120 secs	3
over 120 secs	5
	100

Table 2   Customer service times

Time taken	Frequency
Less than 20 secs	10
20—40 secs	35
40—60 secs	30
60—120 secs	10
over 120 secs	15
	100

customer service times. Begin your simulation at 3 p.m. when there are already three customers in the Post Office, one at each counter. Be explicit as to what assumptions you are making, summarise your results, and suggest what kind of results you would be able to obtain in a full-scale study.

3   Fred's Snax sells tea and sandwiches. Fred does all the service himself, and the time he takes to serve the customers varies in an apparently unpredictable way. Customers arrive at random and queue for service. When served they take their food and drink away with them.

(a)   Draw up an activity cycle diagram for this situation.
(b)   What data would you need to simulate Fred's Snax? How would you collect them?
(c)   Assume you had collected these data and carry out a Monte Carlo simulation study.

4   Repeat assignments (a) — (c) of question 3 for the following situation. Dingle Dairies have a bottling plant with one washing/filling/capping machine. The empty bottles arrive on milk-floats at the plant and are unloaded directly by the milk-float drivers. General labourers then move the vats to the bottle washer where they are loaded manually on to the machine by loading operatives. The bottles emerge clean and filled at the other end of the machine and are automatically loaded and stacked in crates. General labourers then move these crates to the cold store. The following day, the general labourers move the loaded crates from the cold store to the loading bay where the drivers load up their floats and go out on their rounds.

16

The Design of Engineering Facilities at Rover Triumph

A W McCURDY

1   Preliminary survey of the design process

The end objective with any engineering facility is to achieve optimum operating performance defined in terms such as output, cost and quality. The achievement of this objective will depend on

the design of the facility,
the design of control systems to govern its operation,
operational factors, e.g. planned maintenance, material shortages.

The design of the facility and of its operational control systems will, of course, be interdependent and must proceed in parallel. The case study described in this chapter deals with the design of the facility itself. Similar studies were also carried out on the design of the associated control systems.

Adequate design will not be possible unless there are clear and agreed operating performance objectives. Unless such objectives are explicitly defined, it is most unlikely that the facility performance will match that expected. Additionally, there will be no objective criteria with which to compare design alternatives.

To evaluate design alternatives in terms of performance objectives, we need a model which

1   represents the facility structure and connections and also the structure of the control systems;

2   can be readily modified to accept alternatives;
3   can accept dynamic data, such as breakdown probabilities;
4   can be readily manipulated in a dynamic way to predict operational performance.

Until a facility is built and operational it exists only in the form of drawings, specifications, and perhaps a physical model. All these have their uses, but do not completely meet all the above requirements.

It is necessary, therefore, to adopt the simulation approach which involves the development of a logical model. This is not a complete representation of the physical process, but covers those parts of the structure and connections which are directly relevant to the operational objectives. Such a model can be used to evaluate alternative design concepts and to provide valuable quantitative information in identifying areas of the facility and assumed reliability characteristics which have a significant effect on the achievement of performance objectives.

In the case study described below, the model was so large and complex that it had to be constructed in an appropriate simulation language and to be processed on a computer. In this way, many shifts of operation were simulated in a matter of minutes to provide information on the effects on operating performance of changes in the structure of the facility, changes in the reliability of different processes and changes in the operating constraints.

2   The decision to use simulation

Within Rover, the design of engineering facilities was traditionally carried out by the Facilities Planning department. In order to investigate whether facilities were adequate to meet performance objectives, blueprints were used as models of the planning facility together with simple numerical calculations based on average figures for throughputs, rejects, breakdowns, etc. It was felt that these techniques would not be adequate for the planning of the design of a new multi-million pound car body paint shop.

At about that time the simulation approach had been successfully applied by the OR department to a simple facilities design problem, involving the determination of the optimum size of an inter-process buffer. Management were thus aware of the existence and power of the approach. It was agreed that simulation techniques should be used to assist Facilities Planning with the design of the paint shop.

3   Layout of the paint shop

The new paint shop itself was to be a three-storey building with each of the floors connected by a series of automatic lifts. The ground floor was to be a storage area for unpainted bodies (bodies in white) coming from a body assembly area and for painted bodies which had been through the painting processes in the paint shop. The first floor was to contain all the processes which prepare and then paint the body. The second floor contained all the ovens through which bodies have to pass after each preparation and painting process on the first floor.

A consequence of this layout was that each body was involved in 14 transfers between floors by way of the automatic lifts. Since these lifts and also the main processes were subject to breakdown, it was necessary to provide certain buffer storage facilities within the paint shop to minimise the effects of breakdown and also to allow processes to be emptied to avoid damage.

4   Objectives

In discussions between Facilities Planning and Operational Research, the objectives of the study were defined as follows. Given the basic design of the paint shop processes, then in order to ensure the achievement of the planned output of painted vehicle bodies:

1   What size of buffer storage facilities is required?
2   Where should these buffers be located?
3   What should the process track speeds be?

Additionally, it was required (a) to identify processes to which output performance would be sensitive and (b) to study the sensitivity of output to breakdown frequency, with special reference to lifts.

5   Development of the model

A model was set up jointly by Facilities Planning and Operational Research, representing all the significant connections and processes in the paint shop. The size and complexity of the logical model was such as to require the model to be constructed in an appropriate simulation language (General Purpose Simulation System V).

Information was collected on planned track speeds, buffer store sizes and process reject rates. Reliability information for all processes in the paint shop which were liable to breakdown was collected from other paint shops in British Leyland (or from other car manufacturers). This reliability information contained the probability of breakdown per body passing through the process and histograms showing the proportion of such breakdowns falling into different bands of duration. For example, the frequency distribution of breakdown times on lifts and transfers was as follows: 3 mins, 65%; 5 mins, 23%; 10 mins, 8%; 30 mins, 4%.

6   Use of the model

Many shifts of operation were simulated in a matter of minutes on the computer, with varying data to determine the sensitivity of output to changes in paint shop configurations and process track speed and reliability. The model was used as an aid to the design process in collaboration with Facilities Planning over a period of several months.

The type of analysis carried out is illustrated in figure 1. This shows the effect of variations in the reliability of the lifts on achievable output for differing hours of work. For example, working 60 hours a week, only an implausibly low probability of lift stoppage will allow an acceptable output of vehicles. With a 65-hour working week, only an implausibly high stoppage rate will prevent the objective being met. This analysis contributed

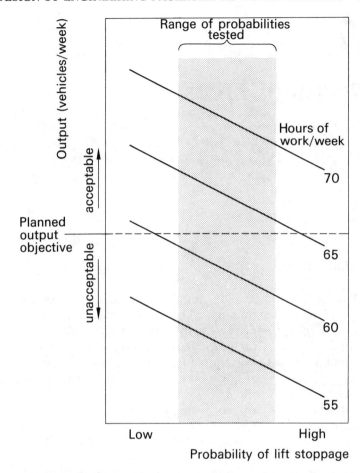

Figure 1. Effect of lift reliability on output for different work levels

to the taking of decisions on maintenance and fall-back procedures for lift operation. Similar analyses were used to determine the location and adequacy of the buffer storage areas.

This application was followed by other studies to investigate the layout and control of the storage areas for 'bodies in white' and painted bodies. Simulation is now in common use in Leyland to assist with the evaluation of changes to existing facilities and the design of new plant.

17

Decision Trees

J B KIDD

1   Introduction

We have now discussed a number of mathematical techniques such as linear programming, inventory control and queueing theory. These provide some assistance in deciding on the optimal amount of each product to manufacture, the volume of finished product to be shipped from each factory to each warehouse, the amount of raw material to carry in stock, the number of machines to provide in a workshop, and so on. All these decisions have two aspects in common. First, they involve a fairly continuous range of choice among alternatives, and similar decisions may be made for hundreds or thousands of products each week. Second, there is either no uncertainty involved or the uncertain events occur sufficiently frequently that they can be measured and handled by probability distributions.

Other decisions do not fit into this pattern. Consider the decisions whether or not to build a new factory, whether to buy a machine of this or that type, whether to launch a new product or spruce up the old one. These are 'either/or' decisions, generally made infrequently on a 'one-off' basis. Moreover, the problem is complicated by uncertainty about the future. It may be that if demand turns out to be high then a new factory will be required, but not if demand turns out to be low. If the factory is to be useful it must be built now before demand is known. How can one decide?

Evidently, this situation involves an element of **choice** on the part of the manager (whether or not to build the factory) and an element of **chance** which is beyond his control (the level of demand). The situation may be more complicated because at some expense and delay the manager could obtain better (but not complete) information about the likely market. If he decides not to build and demand turns out to be high, he can perhaps rent additional capacity or cut back on production elsewhere, whereas if he does build and demand is low he can perhaps sell off or rent out the unwanted capacity. Thus, there is not just one but a series of interactions between choice and chance that need to be considered.

It must be admitted at once that there is no technique available for 'solving' problems of this kind, which are characterised by the interaction between uncertainty and a series of important 'either/or' decisions. What one can do is to lay out the available information in a clear and convenient way, known as a **decision tree,** so that the manager can relatively easily trace out the implications of a particular policy, which corresponds to a particular **branch** of the tree. If the manager or his advisers are prepared to be a little more specific about the probabilities of different eventualities and about their own criteria or objectives, then it may be possible to suggest a 'best' course of action. It is also possible to calculate how much it would be worth paying to acquire additional information, and how one's views and decisions should be modified in the light of this information.

The next chapter describes how Cadbury-Schweppes used decision trees to decide whether or not to test-market a new product before launching it nationally. The problem was that results from test-marketing would give a better idea whether the product should be launched at all, but at the same time would give the competition a chance to step in. Apart from the marketing of new products, decision trees have been used to analyse the purchase of capital equipment, the drilling of oil wells and policy towards research and development. An example used in this chapter concerns whether or not to inspect a sub-assembly before installing it.

2   Elements of a decision

We shall work throughout the chapter with variations of the following problem.

A factory manager named Kahn knows that a certain newly produced sub-assembly may be defective in the sense that if it is installed in the final assembly for which it is intended, the final assembly may fail to function. By submitting the sub-assembly to a very thorough process of complete inspection and hand adjustment, Mr Kahn can make absolutely sure that it will function properly, but this operation will cost £500. On the other hand, if the sub-assembly is installed without being put through this operation and the final assembly fails to function, it will cost £1,000 just to remove and replace the sub-assembly, over and above the £500 it will cost to have it put into a proper condition.

Should Mr Kahn inspect and adjust the sub-assembly before installing it? Intuitively, he should if it is likely to be defective, and should not if it is unlikely to be defective. But what is meant here by 'likely'? What criteria should Mr Kahn use in making his decision?

There are two possible choices for Mr Kahn to make (to inspect or not to inspect), and there are two possible states of the sub-assembly (good or defective), over which he has no control, so there are four possible outcomes to this situation. With each outcome is associated a money cost. The situation may be represented in a simple diagram (figure 1) known as a **pay-off matrix**.

Mr Kahn's decision	State of sub-assembly:	
	Good	Defective
Inspect	£500	£500
Not inspect	0	£1500

Figure 1. Pay-off matrix for Mr Kahn's problem

Three factors are likely to influence Mr Kahn's decision:

1   What are the chances that the sub-assembly is defective?
2   What is his attitude to the risk of unusually high or low costs?
3   Are there other, non-monetary factors which should be taken into account?

Examples of the third factor are public protest at the location of a factory or at the 'exploitation' of labour or certain raw materials, the opposition of unions, other managers or government to a particular course of action, etc. Decision theory cannot say what weight *should* be given to such considerations, but it may well be able to indicate what kind of monetary sacrifice is involved if such considerations are allowed to affect decisions. We shall leave such considerations on one side for the moment.

The second factor is likely to arise when a manager or firm is dealing with financial magnitudes which are very large relative to the magnitudes normally handled. The loss of £250,000 on one project might put a small firm out of business, whereas a large firm could offset such a loss against profits made elsewhere.

Some firms might want to avoid undue risk; others might enjoy taking chances which offer a high reward. In the case described in the next chapter, Cadbury–Schweppes argue that they launch a sufficient number of new products so that the level of profit or loss achieved on any one of them is relatively unimportant. What matters is the overall level of profit over all projects.

In such circumstances it is appropriate to maximise **expected** profit. This is calculated as the profit in each eventuality multiplied by the probability of that eventuality and summed over all possible eventualities. In the present situation it is reasonable to assume that Mr Kahn will take a similar view, and attempt to minimise expected cost. Techniques have been developed for working with the **utility** of money, rather than with money itself, which handle problems of risk to some extent.[8]

Suppose that previous experience has shown that 7 out of 10 of the sub-assemblies are good, i.e. 30% are defective. If Mr Kahn does not inspect, then his cost will be zero with a probability of 0.7 and £1500 with a probability of 0.3. The expected cost of not inspecting is, therefore,

$$(£0 \times 0.7) + (£1500 \times 0.3) = £450$$

This compares with a cost of £500 to inspect. If he wishes to minimise expected cost, Mr Kahn would be advised not to inspect all these sub-assemblies before installation, but rather to remove, adjust and replace those which prove to be defective.

It is quite straightforward to carry out **sensitivity analysis** on this decision. Evidently, if the cost of the inspection were less than £450, then it would be worth inspecting. Similarly, we may calculate how high the probability of a defective sub-assembly would have to be before it would be worth inspecting at a cost of £500. Let the probability of a defective sub-assembly be p, so the probability of a good one is $1 - p$. Then expected cost of not inspecting is

$$£0(1 - p) + £1500 \, (p) = £1500p$$

which is greater than £500 for p greater than one-third. Thus, if 33% or more of the sub-assemblies were defective, it would be cheaper to inspect.

3   Decision trees

The previous problem can alternatively be represented in the form of a decision tree (figure 2) in which square nodes represent points of choice, or decisions, and circle nodes represent points of chance. As time unfolds, one and only one of the branches will be followed. The decision-maker chooses which direction to take at the square nodes, but 'nature' determines the direction at the circle nodes in accordance with the probabilities marked in semi-circles. The cost of each outcome is marked at the end of the appropriate branch. (We do not need to distinguish the quality of the sub-assembly if it is to be inspected anyway, nor need we include the decision to remove, adjust and replace a faulty sub-assembly.)

The decision tree is solved by working *backwards* from the (right-hand) branch tips of the tree, calculating the expected

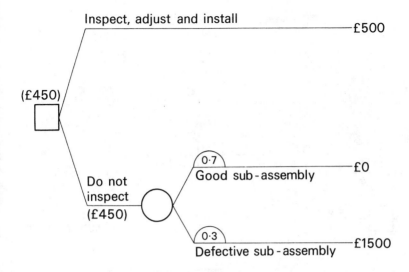

Inspect, adjust and install — £500

(£450)

Do not inspect (£450)

0·7 Good sub-assembly — £0

0·3 Defective sub-assembly — £1500

Figure 2. Decision tree for Mr Kahn's problem

cost for each action and choosing the action with lowest expected cost (assuming that is the appropriate criterion). Thus, we calculate the expected cost of not inspecting as £450 (as before), note this in parentheses by that action, compare it with the cost of £500 to inspect, choose the minimum cost (not inspect £450) and note this at the base of the tree. The result is the same as before, and sensitivity analysis on costs and probabilities can be performed in exactly the same way.

4   Acquisition of new information

The decision tree of the previous example was extremely simple, and did not illustrate the full power of the method to structure complex situations and provide a guide to action. In the present section we shall show how decision trees can be used to analyse the acquisition of new information.

Suppose Mr Kahn can get more information than he now has about the quality of the sub-assembly by subjecting it to a relatively quick test costing £100. This test is not expensive but

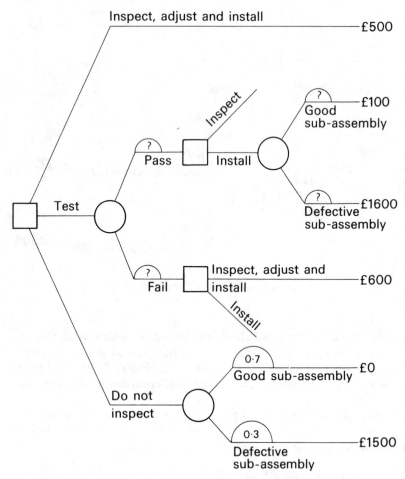

Figure 3. Decision tree incorporating possibility of test

neither is it completely reliable. The engineers have calibrated the test by applying it to several sub-assemblies which were known to be good and to others which were known to be defective. Although most of the good sub-assemblies passed the test and most of the defectives failed, nonetheless some good assemblies failed and some defectives passed. The exact results were as follows.

| Known good sub-assemblies: | 80% passed | 20% failed |
| Known defective sub-assemblies: | 10% passed | 90% failed |

Would Mr Kahn be advised to use this test? The new decision tree may be drawn up as shown in figure 3. It is basically the same as before with the addition of a third alternative corresponding to testing the sub-assembly. The tree has been slightly simplified by assuming that Mr Kahn would not install a sub-assembly which failed the test nor inspect one which passed. (The reader may later check that these are indeed reasonable decisions — see exercise 1a.) But what are the probabilities that the sub-assembly will pass or fail the test? And once the result of the test is known, how should one revise the probabilities of the sub-assembly being good or defective? These new probabilities must be provided before any action can be recommended.

5   Calculation of probabilities

Calculation of the required probabilities is quite possible using the information available. It will help to work with the diagram shown in figure 4 (also used in Moore et al.[5]) Suppose that the square contains one hundred average sub-assemblies. The idea is to sort them into those which are good and those which are defective, and then into those which pass the test and those which fail.

The vertical line divides the 70 good ones from the 30 bad ones, according to the proportions 0.7 and 0.3 experienced by Mr Kahn. Each group is then sub-divided into those that pass and those that fail, according to the proportions found in the calibration tests of the engineers. For example, if 0.7 of the sub-assemblies are good and 0.8 of the good sub-assemblies pass the test, the proportion of total sub-assemblies which both pass the test and are good will be 0.7 x 0.8 = 0.56. The bottom left-hand box will therefore contain 56 of the 100 sub-assemblies. In similar fashion we calculate that the remaining 100 − 56 = 44 sub-assemblies will be divided as follows: 14 good and fail test, 27 defective and fail test and 3 defective and pass test. Expressed as proportions, these numbers are called **joint probabilities** (i.e.

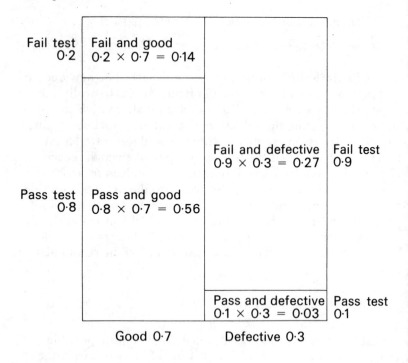

Figure 4. Calculation of conditional probabilities

the probabilities of two 'events' or 'attributes' occurring simultaneously). They are shown in the appropriate boxes of figure 4.

The total number of sub-assemblies which pass the test, whether good or defective, is 56 + 3 = 59; the number which fail is 14 + 27 = 41. Thus, for a sub-assembly chosen at random, the probability it will pass the test is 59/100 = 0.59 (= 0.56 + 0.03), and the probability it will fail is 0.41. This is the first pair of probabilities required for figure 3.

Of the 59 sub-assemblies which pass the test, the proportion 56/59 = 0.95 is good and the remaining proportion 3/59 = 0.05 is defective. Of the 41 which fail the test the proportion 14/41 = 0.34 is good and the remaining proportion 27/41 = 0.66 is defective. These proportions are **conditional probabilities** — the probabilities of the sub-assembly being good or defective conditional upon the result of the test. They show how new information causes the revision of beliefs: in the absence of any other information Mr Kahn should attach a 70% probability to a sub-assembly being defective, but after a test has been carried out he should revise this probability to either 95% or 34% depending upon the result of the test. Mr Kahn still does not have perfect information, but he is now able to make a better guess.

Note that the information provided by the engineers' calibration is also in the form of conditional probabilities — the probability of the test result being conditional upon the quality of the sub-assembly. In effect, we have had to turn these conditional probabilities 'inside-out' to get the ones we need. It is the same information presented in a different form.

A note on terminology is appropriate here. Knowledge and beliefs which exist in the initial situation, before any action is taken, are known as **prior beliefs**; they are conveniently embodied in **prior probabilities**. These beliefs may be based simply on subjective guesses, or upon systematic observations of related phenomena (e.g. the frequency distributions used in the demand forecasting methods discussed in Chapter 10). Once an action has been taken, some new information will generally arise to modify these beliefs and probabilities in some way. The revised probabilities are known as **posterior probabilities**.

We have described in this section a systematic procedure for revising prior probabilities to form posterior probabilities (conditional upon the result of a test). This procedure is based on a theorem due to the eighteenth century philosopher Thomas Bayes. The term **Bayesian** is widely used to refer to procedures of this kind.

6   The decision tree revisited

We have now calculated the required probabilities which may be entered in the decision tree as shown in figure 5. For simplicity, the initial inspect and install decisions have been omitted.

To evaluate the test option, start once more at the right-hand side and 'fold-back'. If the sub-assembly has passed the test and been installed, it will be necessary to replace and adjust it at a cost of £1500 (in addition to the £100 cost of the test) only if

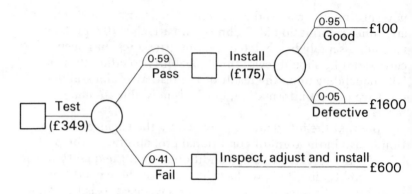

Figure 5. Evaluating the test option

the sub-assembly is defective, which has a (conditional) probability of 0.05. Expected cost if the sub-assembly passes the test is therefore

$$(0.95 \times \pounds100) + (0.05 \times \pounds1600) = \pounds175$$

If the sub-assembly fails the test and is adjusted before installing, the total cost is £100 + £500 = £600. Weighting the cost of each outcome by the probability of that outcome gives the expected cost of the test option as

$$(0.59 \times \pounds175) + (0.41 \times \pounds600) = \pounds349$$

This amount is less than the expected cost of installing directly (£450) or inspecting first (£500). Mr Kahn would therefore be advised to carry out the proposed quick test on all sub-assemblies. If they pass, he should install them, if they fail, inspect and adjust them. His actual cost for any particular sub-assembly will be £100, £600 or £1600, but the average cost over many such sub-assemblies will be £349.

Once again, we may calculate that this quick test would be (just) worthwhile even if it cost another £100, but at any price greater than that it would be cheaper to install sub-assemblies immediately, as before. It would also be possible to calculate by how much the accuracy of the test could be decreased before it would not be worth employing it. The general idea is to show the manager whether the proposed solution is robust, in the sense that it will remain optimal even for large changes in the data and for errors in measurement, or whether one solution rests on a 'knife-edge', in which case some further investigation might be warranted. Finally, one might ask what kind of information would be useful in a problem, and calculate what it would be worth before attempting to obtain the information in some way.

References and further reading

1   Coyle R. G., *Decision Analysis*, Nelson 1972.

2   Lindley D. V., *Making Decisions*, Wiley-Interscience 1971.

3   Magee J. F., 'Decision trees for decision-making', *Harvard Business Review*, July/August, 126, 1964.

4   Magee J. F., 'How to use decision trees in capital investment', *Harvard Business Review*, Sept./October, 70, 1964.

5   Moore P. G., Thomas H., Bunn D. W. and Hampton J. M., *Case Studies in Decision Analysis*, Penguin 1976.

6   Newman J. W., *Management Applications of Decision Theory*, Harper and Row 1971.

7   Raiffa H., *Decision Analysis: Introductory Lectures on Choices Under Uncertainty*, Addison-Wesley 1968.

8   Raiffa H. and Keeney R., *Decisions with Multiple Objectives*, Wiley 1976.

9   Schlaifer R., *Analysis of Decisions Under Uncertainty*, McGraw-Hill 1969.

10   Thompson G. E., *Statistics for Decisions: An Elementary Introduction*, Little Brown Books 1972.

Exercises

1   (a) Complete the decision tree shown in figure 5 by filling in the Inspect and Install branches left incomplete on the test option. Calculate the expected costs of each of these two actions.

(b) In that same example, suppose 50% of the sub-assemblies were defective. Repeat the calculation of the decision tree and advise Mr Kahn how to proceed.

2   A firm is considering whether to build a new factory in order to increase capacity in one line of business. If demand for its product turns out to be high, this action will yield net returns of £250,000. If demand is low there will be a net loss of £100,000. Without further knowledge the company believes that high and low demands are equally likely. However, it can commission a survey of likely customers for a cost of £15,000. In the past the consultants who have carried out such surveys have made correct predictions three quarters of the time when the market has subsequently risen and half the time when the market has subsequently fallen.

(a)   Should the firm commission a survey?
(b)   Should it build a factory?
(c)   How would your answers to these two questions be different if the firm could sell the factory for a loss of only £10,000 in the event of demand turning out to be low?

18
Marketing a New Product at Cadbury Schweppes

R W PIPE

This chapter describes how decision trees were used to help in deciding whether or not to test market before launching a new product. The actual study was carried out at Cadbury Schweppes Ltd in 1967 by Mr D. W. Beattie and was written up as a case study.[1] This chapter draws from the content of that article and, with the benefit of hindsight, comments on the outcome of the study.

1 Introduction

The Company was considering marketing a new product, Aztec, in the chocolate bar section of the highly competitive confectionery market. Consumer tests on samples of product from a small pilot plant had given favourable results. The decision had then to be taken either to put the product on national sale as quickly as possible or to proceed more cautiously by test marketing in a limited region first, to get a better indication of the likely national sale. The former course involved risking large expenditures on plant and promotional activities; the latter approach allowed the collection of additional information before deciding whether to incur the major part of the expenditure, but increased the time before it would become an established profit-making product.

In trying to relate their information to the marketing decision

219

to be made, our market research colleagues felt that there must be a logical way to make the decision. Accordingly, it was decided to try to formulate the problem in terms of a mathematical model.

2   Basic data

The pilot plant was capable of making up to 15 tons per week of the product and the main plant would be capable of making up to a maximum of 120 tons per week, although the capacity was somewhat less than this if conventional shifts were worked. The main plant would cost £100,000 installed and could be in production within one year of the decision to purchase it being made. Initial forecasts were for sales of 70 tons per week (nationally) and the estimators attached a standard error of 20 tons per week to this estimate.

Marketing considerations meant that six months had to be allowed between a decision to launch the product in an area and the introduction date. It was estimated that a test market of at least six months covering part of the country had a three-to-one chance of giving a reliable estimate of the national sales level. Likewise, the level of sale in the first year of national sale had a 90% chance of giving a reliable estimate of the ultimate sales level. In the event of the test market showing the product to be a failure, it would be possible to re-style the product and be ready for a national re-launch two years later. A sales estimate was also given for the re-styled product.

Net contributions (after tax) at various levels of sales for each year forward were also available.

3   Building a model

The first requirement of the model was that it should be capable of solution within the time available. The second was that it should be simple enough for both marketing and operational research personnel to understand and operate. It was therefore decided to draw a decision tree to illustrate the various decisions and possible outcomes.

There were two main alternatives: either to launch nationally as quickly as possible, or to test market in one area only. In the latter case, one would then decide in the light of test results whether to go national as soon as possible thereafter, to drop the idea or to re-style the product entirely. Figure 1 shows the decision tree. To simplify presentation, only the national launch branch is shown in detail. The test market branch is similar but contains an extra year's results and includes the re-styling option, hence is somewhat more complex.

In constructing the tree, the first of several arbitrary decisions had to be made. The sales estimate was given as a mean and a standard error (and was assumed to be distributed normally). For decision purposes, however, a continuous range of outcomes had to be arbitrarily represented as a small number of discrete outcomes. In practice, the distribution was partitioned into three segments (high, medium and low) and the probability and mean value attaching to each segment were calculated.

The criterion adopted for the utility of each course of action was the net present worth. In order to calculate this, the sales contribution, less direct marketing costs, was estimated for each level of sale over the succeeding years, and then the tax payable (in arrears) on these earnings was calculated. This sum was discounted by the appropriate factor (normally the marginal cost of extra capital) to give the net present worth arising from the sale of the product. In the same way, the net present worth of capital expenditure was evaluated, and here the timing of expenditure and the receipt of cash grants needed to be known. The net present worths of earnings under different outcomes are shown at the right-hand side of the model. The capital outlays are omitted for simplicity.

Having represented all the outcomes in the decision tree, the probabilities attaching to each were estimated. The first approach (favoured by our marketing colleagues) was to assess all the probabilities subjectively and then to evaluate each branch of the decision tree by prior analysis. Unfortunately, the subjective assessment of conditional probabilities is notoriously difficult and conditional probabilities abound in this decision tree. Moreover, this approach would not have explicitly used useful information obtained from previous products concerning the reliability of test markets as indicators of final sales. Accordingly, a Bayesian approach was adopted, and the probabilities

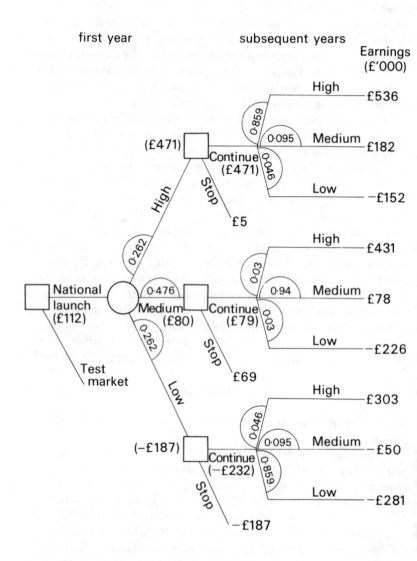

Figure 1. The decision tree – national launch

were calculated by the method described in sections 5 and 6 of the last chapter.

4   Solution and comment on the results

The viability of the new product evidently depends crucially upon the level of sales. In fact, if first year sales are low it is more profitable to stop production than to continue. But there is sufficient chance of medium or high sales to make positive the expected earnings of a national launch.

The expected net present worths of the two alternatives were as follows:

National launch: £112,000 (earnings) less £100,000 (capital outlay), i.e. £12,000.
Test market: £129,000 less £91,000, i.e. £38,000.

The advantage of test marketing over the national launch is £26,000. The decision indicated was to test market and be committed to purchase the plant only if a national sale in the 'high' region were indicated.

Conventional wisdom suggests that test marketing should always be done. Although the case study confirmed this policy in this instance, it can readily be seen that changes in circumstances (e.g. a higher sales estimate) could easily indicate that the loss of revenue in the gap between test market and national extension — to say nothing of competitive activity — could indicate launching a product nationally as quickly as resources permit.

At this point it was interesting to note the effect of the test market. A national launch would only follow the test market if sales in the test market were high. If, however, for 'policy reasons' (e.g. maintaining market share, diversifications, completion of a range, etc.) one were not prepared to kill the product if sales in the mid-region were indicated, this would reduce the value of the test market option. The reduction in net present worth would be £15,000 but test marketing would still be indicated. In this instance, therefore, the first decision was reasonably robust to a subsequent decision being taken in what we have defined as a non-optimal manner.

In addition to the analyses already described, a further analysis was made using a series of modified sales estimates to discover how high the expected level of sale would have to be before a national launch was as valuable an alternative as test marketing first. It was then agreed that to expect a level of sale that high was to be unreasonably optimistic and the decision to test market was confirmed.

From this discussion it will be seen that, in addition to the best course of action being indicated, quite a lot was learned about the effect of possible non-optimal policy decisions and the cost of a range of alternative decisions.

5   Discussion

In using a simple model as this to represent a comparatively complex problem, a number of assumptions and decisions need to be made. It is perhaps useful to consider these, since a proper balance needs to be maintained between simplifying the problem in order to make it manageable and over-simplifying it so that it no longer represents the real-life situation.

(a) **Measures of utility**   In this case the criterion adopted was the net present worth. Although there are disadvantages in equating utility and expected net present worth, in the practical situation it is necessary not only to adopt a method that represents the 'true' utility of each situation but also to convince one's accounting colleagues that it does so.

Other measures of utility, using different accounting methods, or different discount factors are also feasible, as are measures such as brand share. In each case it is important that the measure chosen is the appropriate one for the company and the situation under investigation, otherwise the wrong decision may be made. Utility factors referred to in the previous chapter were considered but rejected on the grounds that average profit was what mattered in the long run in this market, which is dominated by three large companies. Typically, half a dozen new products may be launched each year and it is not expected that all will be winners. However, in the case of a small company, utility factors might well be relevant since no small company could afford the magnitude of loss that might be incurred on any occasion.

(b) Discount factors   Experience in recent years has shown that interest rates and therefore the cost of capital can fluctuate alarmingly, so some form of sensitivity analysis on this factor is desirable. In this particular study, a factor of 10% was taken as the norm and 15% as the highest figure it was felt reasonable to assume at the time (happy days!). However, one fortunate consequence of large discount rates is that events more distant in the future (which are more difficult to predict) are made less significant.

(c) Planning horizon   This was possibly the least satisfactory part of the study, where one is attempting to represent the dynamic marketing situation by an essentially static model. The choice of planning horizon must, to some extent, be arbitrary. The net present worth was calculated on an assumed product life of several years: the stop-go decision process in the model terminated in the second year of national sale and assumed a constant level of sale thereafter. In reality, the product will tend to follow a natural life cycle and opportunities to withdraw the product are always present as are other possibilities (e.g. withdraw advertising support, change the price, etc.).

(d)   Sales estimates   It is necessary to know not only the expected level of sale, but also the distribution about this figure. The determination of this can present problems, but it was overcome by starting from the mean level (which was taken to be the 50/50 point) and asking the forecasters for the 60/40 point (i.e. the level of sale which there is only a 40% chance of exceeding), then the 70/30 point, etc. After some backtracking, a smooth cumulative distribution was eventually built up. This was converted into a frequency distribution, and partitioned as previously described. Further analyses were carried out using different three-way splits and also a four-way split, but the decision to test market remained unaffected (although the advantage over national launch ranged from £26,000 to £34,000).

(e) Choice of model   The model used in this study was unashamedly simple. More complex approaches are available, as discussed in the previous chapter, but one should be wary of giving the data better treatment than they deserve. Project experience suggested that the main advantage of this simple approach was that it lent itself particularly well to construction (and modification) by a group.

In this way the role of the model (and the modeller) is as much to act as a catalyst among the marketing and market research men as to act as a producer of quantitative bases for decisions. Unlike the more complex models, the relationship between these models and the problem is obvious and the element of blind faith correspondingly reduced. Nevertheless, despite its simplicity, it was found that the model still retained the advantages which the discipline of the model building approach brings to a situation. What had been regarded as one large single decision was broken down into a series of smaller decisions and the relationships between these decisions recognised. Thus, the subjective information was refined by the asking of questions that would otherwise have remained unasked. Moreover, the building of the models tended to lead to the use of all the available information. This reduced the very natural tendency for one single factor to have a disproportionate influence on the final decision.

6   Outcome

Evaluating a decision tree is not the same as making a decision. Fortunately, the whole approach to this problem had been worked out from the beginning with market research people and the brand manager. Being to this extent committed to the model, commitment to the decision followed, despite the earlier feeling that an immediate national launch was the best plan. Thus, the decision tree approach proved helpful not merely as a 'black-box' decision-maker, but also as a rational way of relating marketing judgments to the sequential decisions which had to be made.

It is not easy to assess the accuracy of the original subjective probabilities to see whether the right decision was made, since unlikely events do sometimes occur to confound even the best schemes. As it turned out, the initial level of sale after the national launch was above the original estimate, but eventually settled down to a lower level, and thereafter suffered a slow decline. (This life-cycle is typical of many recent products in the confectionery market, which tends to be dominated by a relatively few long stayers such as Cadbury's Dairy Milk and Crunchie.)

This modest history, therefore, tends to vindicate the original decision, for had the product been a high-flier, a decision to test market could, with justification, be heavily criticised; on the other hand, the product did not turn out to be a loss-maker which should have been stifled at birth. At the very least, the study can be said to have clarified the decision-making process in a situation where there was considerable uncertainty.

Reference and further reading

1   Beattie D. W., 'Marketing a new product', *Operational Research Quarterly*, vol. 20, 1969.

19

Putting Operational Research to Work

S L COOK

1 Introduction

Up to now in this book we have covered the background history of OR, the basic idea of its method and approach, a fair range of techniques that have proved useful, and examples of their application. In this last chapter, we turn again to a more general issue, that of how we can 'get it all together' and make it work in our various organisations.

In spite of the many applications listed in these pages, there are difficulties and there have been all too many examples of studies which started in high hope and ended with no successful on-going implementation of a solution to the original problem. This question of 'implementation' has been the subject of considerable research in recent years, and in the ensuing pages we shall discuss some of the most important of these issues.

Of course, no two organisations are exactly alike — they have different sizes, shapes, purposes, styles, and they are made up of unique mixes of unique, individual human beings. Prescriptions and aphorisms are no substitute for experience, common sense and human understanding. We hope the discussions and suggestions of these final pages will be read in that spirit.

2   Roles and responsibilities

There are two main issues in organising the application of OR: the strength of professional support available and the accountability for success of the project. The number of possible combinations is too great to enumerate them all. When discussing the manager 'having a go by himself' we had in mind a situation of little or no professional support; an opposite possibility is where a very strong OR team is given executive responsibility for the project. Both of these possible arrangements have their strengths and uses, but, for reasons of space, we must concentrate here on the more usual situation where there is substantial OR support available, and responsibility is shared in some way between the OR team and the manager.

In the traditional 'line and staff' relationship, the manager retains full authority to make decisions, but must listen to the advice of the 'staff' man, who also has communication channels to higher management through his staff functional links. This is a bureaucratic concept which can work well or badly; in some circumstances both manager and operational researcher may be anxious about their own authority and responsibility. Peter Drucker[10] seeks to resolve this dilemma by recognising the complete authority of the line manager, who must 'carry the can', the staff man being merely an adviser to the manager. Unfortunately this solution recognises neither the amount of interaction needed between operational researcher and manager in an OR project, nor the degree of commitment to results essential to a good operational researcher. An alternative, increasingly acceptable in modern organisations and strongly recommended by many OR men, is to recognise a collective responsibility for the project. Shared responsibility of this kind implies a partnership in which the leadership may move around naturally within the whole team, perhaps from manager to operational researcher to manager again, according to the state of the investigation and the expertise or knowledge most crucial at that stage. There is certainly evidence that natural and effective cooperation of this kind has sometimes been discouraged by over-emphasis on the line manager's authority.

However, there is little doubt either that attempts to increase the authority of the operational researcher through his functional links to higher management can be even more destructive of effective collaboration. The partnership needs to be natural, not imposed.

Thus the manager needs to be able to feel that his partnership with the OR team is one of equals, regardless of how high the OR group reports in the organisation, and how much favour this particular project has in the eyes of top management. He should not be in any doubt that it is this kind of partnership; if through lack of time or experience he feels unable to 'keep his end up' in such a major operation then he can justifiably ask higher management to relieve him of executive responsibility for this particular innovative activity.

3   Modern professional OR function reviewed

In this section we review what an OR function ought ideally to cover, as a sort of yardstick against which efforts in a particular organization might be measured. We do this by grouping the various aspects of OR into five basic 'elements': classical, technical, contextual, dynamic and integrative.

(a) The 'classical' element   This, as its name implies, is the original base from which the eminent founders of OR worked — the base of science, scientific method, and the research approach. It implies curiosity, leading to exploration; the imaginative creation of hypotheses, followed by their ruthless criticism in open debate; intellectual honesty and objectivity.[1,4,7,12]

The classical element brings to a problem a basic mental approach, with certain skills in structuring and handling ideas, including classification and quantification. It also brings an interdisciplinary approach, in which models from a wide range of disciplines may provide analogies which may prove useful in modelling the problem situation. It does not bring any knowledge considered to be specially relevant to the problem situation, but rather an 'open mind' about what is and what is not important.

(b) **The 'technical' element**   This is defined as the skilled application of specific logical and mathematical techniques which can aid problem-solving — a list including all those quantitative techniques described in this book, and many more. Whilst complementary to the classical element in terms of effective OR, it unfortunately demands rather different qualities, temperament and training for its development. This poses problems of balance in the training of the individual in the composition of the group. For example, 'classical' abilities are best developed through experience in a wide range of different problem situations; repeated experience in one problem area is likely to compromise the open mind. Technical abilities, on the other hand, are best developed by repeated experience of using each technique in different, but related, problem areas.

To some extent, it would be possible to have operational researchers, and OR groups, of deliberately different emphasis in order to be suited for different types of work. The emphasis would be on classical OR for unstructured problems of types not yet successfully solved, and 'technical' for relatively standard types of problem. But it is not as simple as that. Even with relatively standard problems, it is often desirable to take a fresh look at the problem; while with unstructured problems, progress can especially be made by separating out parts of the problem which are amenable to standard techniques in order to reveal more clearly the essential kernel of the problem for attack by the more 'classical' approach. So the two elements are very much complementary in good OR and must be developed in the same group and as far as possible in the same individuals.

A most important skill is the ability to generate and develop new techniques (logical and quantitative) needed by many problems. This skill is perhaps on the borderline between the classical and the technical elements.

(c) **The 'contextual' element**   This is defined here as the application of relevant existing theory and of relevant practical experience, from areas of knowledge specific to the context of the problem. This contrasts with both the classical and the technical elements. The emphasis of OR has always been to study the problem as it is, in its context, from what can be measured and observed in that context. Relationships built into the model have, as far as possible, been derived from observation of the problem context, rather than inferred from general theory.

But there have always been exceptions to this. In the earliest OR, where a problem involved natural science or engineering phenomena, technological relationships based on theory were often incorporated as, for example, in the early U-boat studies. Even where the knowledge is of a very empirical kind — such as experience of success and failure of particular practices in a field such as, say, traffic management — it can provide useful guidelines in approaching a problem.

(d) The 'dynamic' or 'change agent' element   All three elements described so far have been concerned with selecting the best or most appropriate solution to the stated problem, i.e. with deciding upon the desirable new state of the system. This is a 'static' concept, but successful implementation involves moving from the present to the new state — a dynamic process. However desirable the proposed new state to all concerned, the road to it from the present state may be unacceptably rough, or it may need special navigational aids.

Some of the issues involved in successful implementation of OR results have already been discussed in section 2. These were mainly the issues of manager/scientist collaboration which is part of the problem. With any major change there are much broader issues of acceptability to all concerned — workers, customers, citizens; and here managers and scientists alike may need help, not to manipulate people into acceptance, but to set up the kinds of genuine participation in problem-solving that can lead naturally to acceptance.

Here we can draw on some of the ideas, approaches and experience of those behavioural scientists who have been concerned with programmes of social change in organizations, typified, for example by Professor Warren Bennis.[3] These people, often self-designated as 'change agents' in recent years, usually concentrate their analysis on the behavioural factors in the organizational situation — with *how* the people interact rather than *what* people are trying to do. OR by contrast has normally been concerned with the efficient performance of the tasks of the organization and only incidentally with the human interactions involved. It seems likely that in the future these problems will yield best to combined study of both the 'task' and 'inter-personal' aspects, so that a combination of OR and behavioural change agents skills will be needed.

(e) The 'integrative' element   Finally, we come to the integrative element in OR; not just the ability to combine ideas and concepts from various disciplines, or the ability to combine theory with action — both of these are implied in other elements — but the ability to combine the activities to achieve a result in line with the needs of the situation — cost, timeliness, perhaps even style. We are concerned with the skills of the project leader and project manager in achieving the right balance of effort within and between the other four elements. Experience is especially important here. There is little doubt that in this element, art predominates over science, although there are some semi-scientific aids to project management that can be usefully applied.

It must be very clear by now that no operational researcher can be a self-contained 'jack of all trades'. That would be hard enough to achieve even within one of the elements, let alone across the five. All we can hope for in the individual is a degree of special competence in some parts of some of the elements and a general awareness of the remainder. Thus, a problem of any complexity needs to be tackled by a team of interactive individuals who together have a reasonable level of ability in the most important aspects; the project team needs to be backed up by a well-balanced OR group, backed up in turn by the profession as a whole and by the whole network of relevant knowledge and skills.

This, then, is the 'ideal' role of modern operational research, although not all organizations will find it necessary to exploit the full scope of OR.

4   Identifying worthwhile projects and selecting appropriate techniques for their solution

In this chapter we have discussed so far the roles of managers and of operational researchers in applying OR, the conditions for successful implementation of solutions and the nature of an effective OR group. We must leave for another place the problems of how to fit the group into the organisation structure and how to manage and control OR work within the organisation. One question remains to be tackled here: what should the group actually do? More precisely, how are possible projects identified, and how is it decided what techniques to use for a project?

Projects can be identified and selected for study in a wide variety of ways. When one new OR group was set up, the newly appointed manager made a six-week tour of the seven operating divisions, discussing the main problems being faced with general managers and their middle managements. From this came a list of 24 possible problems for OR. In discussion with the managing director's advisory committee, four of these were selected for study. Of these, three yielded good cash savings, two of them very substantial; the fourth was unsuccessful. Overall, the savings directly attributable to the OR work represented a return of about 200% per annum on the total project costs; the best projects reached a figure of 500% per annum. As a result, the group was expanded and a rule of thumb was devised that in future no 'bread and butter' projects would be taken on unless there was clear scope for at least a 500% saving. It was recognised that some of the most important OR projects would have intangible benefits or very uncertain outcomes, and that these must be exempted from this calculation. As a safeguard, however, there should always be enough 'bread and butter' projects to yield tangible returns that can more than pay for the group's total activity.

Once a group is successfully launched, there is usually no point in further general surveys for potential projects — they will arise continually and the problem will be selecting those to be undertaken. Sometimes an urgent call for short-term help from management may lead to results revealing scope for major studies (one 10-day emergency study led to a two-year project yielding improvements worth £200,000 per annum). Conversely, a six-man year investigation requested by the managing director to assist the board with long-range strategic decisions, led also to a series of worthwhile operational improvements and a major computer scheme.

Quite often, sucessful completion of an OR study in one

section of an organisation will lead to studies in neighbouring parts; for example, a stock control study for finished goods may lead forward to marketing or back into production control problems. And yet another source of profitable OR work, paradoxically, can be a survey of the opportunities to apply a particular technique, perhaps newly acquired within the group, which catches the imagination of the managers. Normally, 'technique-orientation' should be avoided like the plague — the focus should be on the problem and the technique should be incidental. But when some years ago one group set one of its newly recruited scientists to explore the scope for using linear programming to reduce iron and steel making costs, hitherto unrecognised problems were identified and very considerable benefits achieved first in one division and then in two others. An occasional technique-oriented exercise like this, carried out by a clearly problem-oriented group can thus be very effective.

In most projects, the problem will be identified and the study commenced before any attempt is made to consider which techniques will be relevant. However, a choice of technique has to be made in due course, and students and new practitioners often ask 'how do you decide what techniques to use?' The question is unfortunately almost impossible to answer. There is not much that can replace a gradual acquisition of experience and of the art of OR problem solving. Clearly, a study of past case histories can help speed up this acquisition, whilst, given a particular case, discussion with others who have successfully tackled similar problems can help. In some cases the choice may be obvious; in others it may pay to explore different technique options in parallel before deciding which to use.

As a very general guide, however, we can set out roughly the extent to which groups of techniques have been used with success in industrial OR groups over the past 20 years. These groups are listed in descending order of frequency of use, of the group as a whole, judged on a very approximate subjective basis. In each group, elementary techniques are mentioned first, then more advanced ones (which may be used relatively infrequently). The dotted line represents a rough cut-off point below which it can be said that the techniques, whilst they may give useful insight, are only rarely instrumental in solving a real-world problem.

1   Cost models, relating cost in money terms algebraically to various physical and behavioural variables: from 'standard costing' representations to cost effectiveness and cost benefit analysis.

2   Statistical methods: from sampling and correlation and regression to statistical quality control, design of experiments and time series.

3   Simulation (representing interacting events in a complex system through time): from simple activity analysis charts to probabilistic computer representations — sometimes the 'Monte Carlo method — and man-machine simulations or operational exercises where there is human intervention in an interaction with the computer run; also 'systems dynamics' (non-probabilistic computer representation of very complex systems with internal feedbacks) e.g. world modelling.

4   Mathematical programming: from linear programming to non-linear (e.g. quadratic, integer, dynamic and goal-programming).

5   Network methods: from critical path analysis and resource allocation for optimal project control and completion to vehicle routing and graph theory.

6   Inventory theory: from simple rules for re-order level and re-order quantity to complex probabilistic models with automatic updating of parameters, specification of review procedures, demand forecasting and smoothing, etc. (see also 2 above).

7   Decision analysis: from simple deterministic decision trees to probabilistic ones, weighting of outcomes, maximisation of utilities.

. . . .

8   Reliability theory (timing of machine replacements).

9   Queueing theory (used for simple queueing situations).

10   Game theory, conflict analysis, conflict resolution.

11   Search theory.

This list should of course be taken only as a very rough guide; and there are considerable overlaps between some of the categories, as well as some omissions. As the OR staff develop some experience, that experience will take over in guiding their choice of techniques and for them a list of this kind will have little purpose.

5   Epilogue

This last chapter has tried to select a few pointers towards the establishment of a worthwhile OR function in an organisation. As with most activities there is a limit to the value of prescription; trial and error is unavoidable. Perhaps we could just emphasise in a few words the qualities needed in a good OR group. In addition to intellectual competence, they should have (and should be encouraged by the organisation to have): enthusiasm; curiosity as to how the organisation ticks; intellectual honesty; an achievement orientation; a healthy scepticism of accepted ideas and practice; and a deep commitment *both* to science and to the organisation.

After this emphasis on the setting up of a formal OR function, perhaps we could return finally to the point we made in Chapter 1. This book is addressed mainly to managers and potential managers as individuals rather than to organisations. The individual manager may be in no position, as yet, to influence the setting up of an OR group in his organisation; or there may already be one there, but not available in his sector. We hope this book may have given him some support for doing some OR himself. If he does, we hope the book will also encourage him to keep in touch with the OR community, and perhaps even suffer vicariously from its failures and enjoy its successes as it continues to try to expand its competence and its applications in the world at large.

References and further reading

1   Ackoff R. L., *Scientific Method: Optimising Applied Research Decisions*, Wiley 1962.

2   Argyris C., 'Today's problems with tomorrow's organisations', *Journal of Management Studies*, vol. 4, no. 1, February 1967.

3   Bennis W. G., 'Organisational change', Chapter 5 of Lawrence J. R. (ed.), *Operational Research and the Social Sciences*.

4   Bronowski J., *The Common Sense of Science*, Penguin 1960.

5   Burns T. and Stalker G. M., *The Management of Innovation*, Tavistock 1961.

6   Churchman C. W. and Schainblatt A. H., 'The Researcher and the manager: a dialectic of implementation' and 'Commentary', *Management Science*, February 1965, and October 1965.

7   Churchman C. W., *Prediction and Optimal Decision: Philosophical Issues of a Science of Values*, Prentice-Hall 1961.

8   Cook S. L., 'Purpose and quality of graduate education in the management sciences', *Management Science*, vol. 17, no. 2, October 1970.

9   Cook S. L., 'Scientific approaches to business problems, or the advancement of science in management', Chapter 5 of Hugh-Jones E. M. (ed.), *Economics and Technical Change*, Blackwell 1969.

10   Drucker P., *The Practice of Management*, Heinemann 1960, pp. 292–6, Pan 1968.

11   Likert R., *New Patterns of Management*, McGraw-Hill 1961.

12   Magee B., *Popper*, Fontana 1973.

13   Mant A., 'Management education in the 1970's', *Management Education Conference*, British Institute of Management 1970.

14   McGregor D., *The Human Side of Enterprise*, McGraw-Hill 1960.

15   Morris W. T., *Management Science in Action*, Irwin 1963.

Appendix 1

Area under the normal density function: a table of

$$\Phi(x) = \frac{1}{\sqrt{2\pi}} \int_{-\infty}^{x} e^{-\frac{1}{2}y^2} \, dy$$

x	0.00	0.01	0.02	0.03	0.04	0.05	0.06	0.07	0.08	0.09
0.0	.5000	.5040	.5080	.5120	.5160	.5199	.5239	.5279	.5319	.5359
0.1	.5398	.5438	.5478	.5517	.5557	.5596	.5636	.5675	.5714	.5753
0.2	.5793	.5832	.5871	.5910	.5948	.5987	.6026	.6064	.6103	.6141
0.3	.6179	.6217	.6255	.6293	.6331	.6368	.6406	.6443	.6480	.6517
0.4	.6554	.6591	.6628	.6664	.6700	.6736	.6772	.6808	.6844	.6879
0.5	.6195	.6950	.6985	.7019	.7054	.7088	.7123	.7157	.7190	.7224
0.6	.7257	.7291	.7324	.7357	.7389	.7422	.7454	.7486	.7517	.7549
0.7	.7580	.7611	.7642	.7673	.7704	.7734	.7764	.7794	.7823	.7852
0.8	.7881	.7910	.7939	.7967	.7995	.8023	.8051	.8078	.8106	.8133
0.9	.8159	.8186	.8212	.8238	.8264	.8289	.8315	.8340	.8365	.8389
1.0	.8413	.8438	.8461	.8485	.8508	.8531	.8554	.8577	.8599	.8621
1.1	.8643	.8665	.8686	.8708	.8729	.8749	.8770	.8790	.8810	.8830
1.2	.8849	.8869	.8888	.8907	.8925	.8944	.8962	.8980	.8997	.9015
1.3	.9032	.9049	.9066	.9082	.9099	.9115	.9131	.9147	.9162	.9177
1.4	.9192	.9207	.9222	.9236	.9251	.9265	.9279	.9292	.9306	.9319
1.5	.9332	.9345	.9357	.9370	.9382	.9394	.9406	.9418	.9429	.9441
1.6	.9452	.9463	.9474	.9494	.9495	.9505	.9515	.9525	.9535	.9545
1.7	.9554	.9564	.9573	.9582	.9591	.9599	.9608	.9616	.9625	.9633
1.8	.9641	.9649	.9656	.9664	.9671	.9678	.9686	.9693	.9699	.9706
1.9	.9713	.9719	.9726	.9732	.9738	.9744	.9750	.9756	.9761	.9767
2.0	.9772	.9778	.9783	.9788	.9793	.9798	.9803	.9808	.9812	.9817
2.1	.9821	.9826	.9830	.9834	.9838	.9842	.9846	.9850	.9854	.9857
2.2	.9861	.9864	.9868	.9871	.9875	.9878	.9881	.9884	.9887	.9890
2.3	.9893	.9896	.9898	.9901	.9904	.9906	.9909	.9911	.9913	.9916
2.4	.9918	.9920	.9922	.9925	.9927	.9929	.9931	.9932	.9934	.9936
2.5	.9938	.9940	.9941	.9943	.9945	.9946	.9948	.9949	.9951	.9952
2.6	.9953	.9955	.9956	.9957	.9959	.9960	.9961	.9962	.9963	.9964
2.7	.9965	.9966	.9967	.9968	.9969	.9970	.9971	.9972	.9973	.9974
2.8	.9974	.9975	.9976	.9977	.9977	.9978	.9979	.9979	.9980	.9981
2.9	.9981	.9982	.9982	.9983	.9984	.9984	.9985	.9985	.9986	.9986
3.0	.9987	.9987	.9987	.9988	.9988	.9989	.9989	.9989	.9990	.9990
3.1	.9990	.9991	.9991	.9991	.9992	.9993	.9992	.9992	.9993	.9993
3.2	.9993	.9993	.9994	.9994	.9994	.9994	.9994	.9995	.9995	.9995
3.3	.9995	.9995	.9995	.9996	.9996	.9996	.9996	.9996	.9996	.9997
3.4	.9997	.9997	.9997	.9997	.9997	.9997	.9997	.9997	.9997	.9998
3.6	.9998	.9998	.9999	.9999	.9999	.9999	.9999	.9999	.9999	.9999

Appendix 2

Demand analysis/forecasting worksheet (Exercises 2 and 3, p. 127)

1	Current demand value	d_t	60
2	Forecast	u_{t-1}	30*
3	Error	$e_t = d_t - u_{t-1}$	
4	Cumulative error	Σe_t	
5	Squared error	e_t^2	
6	Cumulative squared error	Σe_t^2	
7	$\alpha \times$ error	αe_t	
8	$(1-\alpha)$ past smoothed error	$(1-\alpha)\bar{e}_{t-1}$	1*
9	Current smoothed error	$\bar{e}_t = \alpha e_t + (1-\alpha)\bar{e}_{t-1}$	
10	$\alpha \times$ absolute error	$\alpha \mid e_t \mid$	
11	$(1-\alpha)$ past MAD	$(1-\alpha)\text{MAD}_{t-1}$	3*
12	Current MAD	$\text{MAD}_t = \alpha \mid e_t \mid + (1-\alpha)\text{MAD}_{t-1}$	
13	Current std dev	$1.25 \times \text{MAD}_t$	
14	Tracking signal	$T_t = \bar{e}_t / \text{MAD}_t$	
15	Exponential weighting constant for forecast† (see below)	A	
16	$A \times$ current demand	Ad_t	
17	$(1-A) \times$ past forecast	$(1-A)u_{t-1}$	
18	Next month's forecast	$u_t = Ad_t + (1-A)u_{t-1}$	

†Simple exponential smoothing $A = \alpha$, adaptive response rate forecasting $A = \mid T_t \mid$,
*Estimate or guess

75	75	60	75	65	70	77	60		

elayed adaptive response rate forecasting $A = |\, T_{t-1}\,|$.

Index